JESUS WAS A BILLIONAIRE

BREAKING THE CURSE OF BEING BROKE

---◆---

ALLAN SEALY

LIFE AND SUCCESS PUBLISHING
Publishers of Inspiration

Copyright © Allan Sealy 2021
www.allansealy.com

All rights reserved. No part of this publication may be produced, distributed, or transmitted in any form or by any means, including photocopying, recording, or other electronic or mechanical methods, without the prior written permission of the publisher, or except in the case of brief quotations embodied in critical reviews and certain other noncommercial uses permitted by copyright law.
For permission requests, write to the publisher, addressed
"Attention: Permissions Coordinator" at the email address below

Life and Success Media Ltd
email info@abookinsideyou.com
www.abookinsideyou.com

This book is sold subject to the condition that it may not be resold or otherwise issued except in its original binding. The CIP catalogue record for this book is available from the British Library. British Library Cataloguing-in-Publishing Data. Unless otherwise stated all scripture quotations are taken from the Holy Bible New King James Version. Quotations marked NKJV are taken from the
HOLY BIBLE NEW KING JAMES VERSION.
Copyright © 1973 1978 1984 by International Bible Society.
Used by permission of Hodder and Stoughton Ltd a member of the Hodder Headline Plc Group. All rights reserved. "NKJV" is a registered trademark of International Bible Society. UK trademark number 1448790. Quotations marked KJV are from the Holy Bible
King James Version.

ISBN: 978-1-7398859-9-1
Cover design & layout by
MIADESIGN.COM

Contents

Special Note

Book 1
Young Gifted and Rich [7]

Foreword

1. God v Money [15]
2. Christ v Christianity [25]
3. The Profile of God's Leading Servants [41]
4. The Grace of Our Lord Jesus Christ [51]
5. Confronting The Virtues of Poverty [55]
6. Born into Wealth [67]
7. A Tribute for The King [79]
8. JESUS: Young, Gifted and Rich [87]

Book 2
Mind Before Matter [103]

9. The Lesson for the Rich Young Ruler [115]
10. Beware the leaven of the Pharisees [121]
11. Where Is Your Treasure? [135]
12. The Spirit of Wisdom [145]
13. Manifesting The Father [155]
14. The Lesson for the Rich Young Ruler [163]
15. Take Up Your Cross [173]

Book 3
Good Success [179]

16. Milk and Honey [185]
17. Divine Rest [191]
18. Manifesting Finished Works [199]
19. The Good that You Desire [203]
20. How Good Do You Want God to Be? [207]
21. Your Divine Identity demands for you to be Rich [219]
22. Honor The Lord with Wealth [223]
23. Don't be on the Wayside [231]
24. Get Behind Me, Satan [237]

The Decision [253]

DEDICATION

This Book is dedicated to
my daughters, Jasmin & Jada.
I love you both deeply.

SPECIAL THANKS

I want to give special thanks to:

My Dad (The Wise One)
- for your wisdom, love and guidance -

My Mother (My Rock)
- for your unfailing love and sacrifice -

SUPREME THANKS

My supreme thanks to:

My Heavenly Father,
The Lord Jesus Christ
& The Holy Spirit

through whom all things are possible

SPECIAL NOTE

This book was not written to limit Jesus to any monetary value but to denounce the idea that our Lord and Saviour was poor or even the poorest of the poor. Jesus' earthly ministry took place in a time and place where material prosperity often served as an indicator of one's spiritual well-being. According to the Torah and Mosaic law, adherence to the commandments was believed to result in living under an *"Open Heaven,"* leading to a life of prosperity. Conversely, poverty was seen as evidence of living under a *"Brass heaven,"* suggesting disobedience. This societal perspective led to the mistreatment of the poor in ancient Judean society, with the *"very poor"* even being excluded from participating in religious ceremonies.

For Christ to be presented as the "spotless sacrificial lamb" for humanity's redemption, He needed to be beyond reproach in terms of fulfilling the law. Additionally, He required unrestricted access to the temple, where He began teaching from a young age. Both of these requirements were met through factors such as wealth and prosperity, among other things, as it was crucial for all to clearly see that He lived under an "Open Heaven."

What truly set Jesus apart from other affluent Rabbis in His society was His compassion for and interaction with the poor, as opposed to passing judgment or stigmatizing them. He offered them the grace that the law could not provide—an unmerited favor that granted both spiritual and material prosperity, allowing them access to the boundless resources of His Kingdom and the opportunity to partake in the divine nature.

Out of all the virtues of Christ, it was His material wealth and abundance that the Holy Spirit used to symbolize His grace. This is why Paul wrote:

For you know the grace of our Lord Jesus Christ, that though He was rich, yet for your sakes He became poor, that you through His poverty might become rich.
(2 Corinthians 8:9)

This is but one of the great exchanges of virtue that took place *'on the cross,'* where Christ took on our poverty that we might become rich.

BOOK 1
YOUNG GIFTED AND RICH

FOREWORD
THE REAL JESUS CHRIST

        The common concept of Christ was given to the church by the priests of the dark ages, at a time when a religious ideal was wanted which should induce men to be content with slavery, and to bow their necks to every kind of wrong and oppression; and this concept was drawn almost wholly from the poetry of Isaiah; the Christ of the churches is the Christ of Isaiah, and our ideas of

Him are not drawn at all from an impartial study of the history of His life. Such passages in the prophecies as;

"He is despised and rejected of men; a man of sorrows and acquainted with grief; and we hid, as it were, our faces from him; he is brought as a lamb to the slaughter, and as a sheep before her shearers is dumb, so he opened not his mouth,"

have been quoted to show His character, and the meekness and humbly submissive spirit with which He endured wrong and injustice. We have had held up as the ideal man a despised, friendless, poverty-stricken laborer whom the upper classes regarded with scorn because of his lowly origin and station; who had no friends save fishermen, laborers, outcasts and sinners; who was often shirtless and hungry, and who bore insults and persecutions with meek submission, and walked about in a scornful world with his hands always uplifted in loving benediction.

This character has too long been offered as the Christian ideal;

- **Be meek,**
- **Be submissive,**
- **Be lamb-like or sheep-like.**

Bow your head before the persecutor, and offer your back to the shearer. Rejoice when you are fleeced; it is for the glory of God. It is a good religion *for the man with the shears.*

The Christ who was held up in the old-fashioned orthodox pulpit is a weak character. He is not the kind of a man we would nominate for president, and his followers have very little faith in Him as an organizer. No railroad magnate of today would make Him foreman of a section; and if it were broadcast over the country tonight that the president of the United States had resigned and that Jesus would be inaugurated tomorrow, 95 percent of the Christians there would draw their money out of the banks for fear Jesus might start a panic.

What we propose to do now is to ascertain by a study of the four gospels in the light of history whether this is the real Christ; and if not, to find what the real Christ was like.

In the first place, Jesus could not have been despised because He was a carpenter, or the reputed son of a carpenter. Custom required every Jewish Rabbi or teacher to have a trade. We read in the Talmud of Rabbi Johanan, the blacksmith, and of Rabbi Isaac, the shoemaker, learned and highly honored men. Rabbi Jesus, the carpenter, would be spoken of in the same way. St. Paul, a very learned man, was a tent-maker by trade. At that time, and among that people, Jesus could not have been despised for His birth and station. He was popularly supposed to be of royal blood, being saluted as the son of David; His lineage was well known. The people who cried *"Hosannah to the son of David"* knew that He was an aristocrat of the aristocrats; a prince of the royal house. He was not *"lowly"* in birth, nor was He supposed to be so.

HE WAS EDUCATED

Second, He could not have been despised for His ignorance, for He was a very learned man. Whenever He went into a synagogue, He was selected to read the law and teach the congregation, as the one best qualified for that work. Luke says; *"There went a fame of Him through all the region round about, and He taught in their synagogues, being glorified of all."* In those times of fierce religious disputation, no unlearned man could have held his own in such fashion. He must have been letter-perfect in the books of the Jewish law, for He was always able to rout His adversaries by making apt quotations from their own books. Even His enemies always addressed Him as Master, or Teacher, acknowledging His profound learning.

JESUS HAD PLENTY

Third, He was not despised for His poverty, for He had many wealthy and influential friends, and knew no lack of anything. Lazarus and his sisters, whose home was always open to Him, were people of consequence; for we are told that "many of the Jews" came to comfort the sisters when Lazarus died.

Luke says that Joanna, the wife of Chuza, the king's steward, and other women **"ministered unto him of their substance;"** that is, they were supporters of His work.

The king's steward was a high official, and his wife would be a prominent lady.

Joseph of Arimathea, who came to get the body of Jesus, was a well-to-do man. So, probably was Nicodemus.

Jesus healed the sick in the families of rulers and high officials, and they appear to have responded liberally in supplying His financial needs.

He dressed expensively, lived well and never lacked for money. When He was crucified, the soldiers cast lots for His clothing because it was too fine to cut up, as they would have done with the garments of an ordinary man; and on the night of His betrayal, when Judas went out, it was supposed by the others that he had gone to give something to the poor. It must have been their custom to give away money, or how could such a supposition have arisen?

In that country and climate, the wants of Jesus and His disciples were few and simple, and they seem to have been fully supplied. He wore fine clothes, had plenty to eat and drink, and had money to give away.

JESUS WAS NOT HUMBLE

Fourth, Jesus was not humble, in the commonly accepted meaning of the word. He was a man of the most impressive, commanding and powerful personal appearance. He "spoke as one having authority" and "His word was with power."

Frequently, we are told, great fear and awe fell upon the people at His mighty words and works. In one place they were so frightened that they besought Him to leave; and John tells how certain officers sent to arrest Him in the market place lost their nerve in His commanding presence, and went back, saying:

"Surely, never man spake like this man."

On the night of His arrest a band of soldiers approached Him in the grove and asked for Jesus of Nazareth; and when He answered "I am he," such was His majesty and power that they prostrated themselves; "they went backward," the account says, "and fell to the ground."

- John 18:6

To be like the Christ of the four Gospels, one must be learned, well dressed, well supplied with money, and of noble and commanding appearance, speaking with authority, and having tremendous magnetic power.

Wallace Wattles
Author of The Science of Getting Rich

CHAPTER 1
GOD VS MONEY

"No one can serve two masters; for either he will hate the one and love the other"

In 1867, Charles Spurgeon *(known as the 'prince of preachers')*, delivering a sermon to the then largest church congregation in Christendom, said,

"I believe that it is anti-Christian and unholy for any Christian to live with the object of accumulating wealth. You will say, 'Are we not to strive all we can to get all the money we can?' You may do so. I cannot doubt but what, in so doing, you may do service to the cause of God. But what I said was that to live with the object of accumulating wealth is anti-Christian."

Saint Josemaria Escriva, founder of the Catholic organization - Opus Dei, was asked in an interview to comment on the virtue of poverty in view of increasing social awareness in society. Here is an excerpt from what he said,

"The poor will have the Gospel preached to them' (Matthew 11:6).

We read in Scripture, precisely as one of the signs which mark the arrival of the Kingdom of God. Those who do not love and practice the virtue of poverty do not have Christ's spirit. This holds true for everyone. For the hermit who retires to the desert; and for the ordinary Christian who lives among his fellow men, whether he enjoys the use of this world's resources or is short of many of them."

St. Augustine's doctrine of charity became the heart of Christian thought and practice. Augustine portrayed the Christian pilgrimage toward the heavenly city by analogy to a traveler's journey home.

"The city of God, humankind's true home, is characterized by the love of God even to the contempt of self, whereas the earthly city is characterized by the love of self even to the contempt of God. It is the goal—not the journey—that is important. The world and its goods may be used for the journey, but if they are enjoyed, they direct the traveller away from God to the earth."

So I ask you...

> **"IS IT GREEDY OR ANTI-CHRISTIAN TO EARN MUCH MORE THAN YOU (AND YOUR FAMILY) NEED TO LIVE ON?"**

> **"IS IT REALLY AGAINST THE SPIRIT OF CHRIST NOT TO PRACTICE THE VIRTUE OF POVERTY?"**

> **"WOULD THE ENJOYMENT OF MATERIAL WEALTH REALLY STEER YOU AWAY FROM GOD?"**

Although these questions have a moral value attached to them, ultimately, they are derived from a particular perception concerning God and money. As a result, there is a great amount of ambivalence within the church, on the subject of money and the possession of material wealth. So much so, that Christianity seems to be polarized into two main camps:

Those who are hyper-prosperity, believing that being prosperous is the unequivocal indicator of God's favor and blessings in one's life.

Versus

Those who vehemently condemn the theology of prosperity, deeming it among the most destructive heresies throughout the history of the Church.

Amidst these extremes, there exists a middle ground occupied by those who, while not opposed to the concept of prosperity, advocate for a more restrained form of it, with a *low* ceiling! So, who's right? Who's wrong? More importantly, who has God's divine stamp of approval?

To address this issue, let's talk about mammon.

MAMMON

"No one can serve two masters; for either he will hate the one and love the other, or else he will be loyal to the one and despise the other. You cannot serve God and mammon."

- Matthew 6:24

While the term *"mammon"* is often used to denote 'money,' 'the personified embodiment of money,' or even, in more extreme cases, 'the malevolent spirit of money,' its primary connotation pertains to the *influence* of money. Influence, by definition, is the capacity to affect the character, development, or behavior of someone. That being the case, mammon is more *psychological* than physical. The physical counterpart of money has no intrinsic value. It is just cheap paper and metal coins. Its value only lies in it being an *'accepted'* medium of exchange for goods, services, and time. That acceptance is the *spiritual* aspect of money, which is where its influence lies. From now on, when the words money or mammon are mentioned in this book, I want to you to think of it as a **form of influence**.

Prior to saying you cannot serve God and mammon, Jesus shared the story of the *'unjust steward,'* setting the tone and context for His statement about money.

"There was a certain rich man who had a steward, and an accusation was brought to him that this man was wasting his goods. So he called him and said to him, 'What is this I hear about you? Give an account of your stewardship, for you can no longer be steward.' Then the steward said within himself, 'What shall I do? For my master is taking the

stewardship away from me. I cannot dig; I am ashamed to beg. I have resolved what to do, that when I am put out of the stewardship, they may receive me into their houses.'

So, he called every one of his master's debtors to him, and said to the first, 'How much do you owe my master?' And he said, 'A hundred measures of oil.' So he said to him, 'Take your bill, and sit down quickly and write fifty.' Then he said to another, 'And how much do you owe?' So he said, 'A hundred measures of wheat.' And he said to him, 'Take your bill, and write eighty.' So the master commended the unjust steward because he had dealt shrewdly. For the sons of this world are more shrewd in their generation than the sons of light.

And I say to you, make friends for yourselves by unrighteous mammon, that when you fail, they may receive you into an everlasting home. He who is faithful in what is least is faithful also in much; and he who is unjust in what is least is unjust also in much. Therefore, if you have not been faithful in the unrighteous mammon, who will commit to your trust the true riches?

- Luke 16:1-11

While Jesus characterized mammon as *'unrighteous,'* He wholeheartedly endorsed the use of it! This sentiment is reflected in the case of the *unjust* steward. Faced with the threat of losing his livelihood, the steward leveraged the influence of money to secure his future well-being - which incidentally resulted in benefits for his employer. Remarkably, not only was the steward praised for his actions, but his handling of *'unrighteous mammon'* served as an example of why,

"The children of this world are in their generation wiser than the children of light."

- Luke 16:8 KJV

"BUT WHY WOULD JESUS ENDORSE THE USE OF SOMETHING HE CALLS UNRIGHTEOUSNESS?"

To answer this question, let us first define what righteousness is. Righteousness is a complex word with multiple definitions and usages. These definitions include:

- The quality of being morally right or justifiable
- To act according to moral or divine law
- To be free from guilt or sin
- To make right decisions
- Doing what is right
- The quality of being right in God's eyes

I believe a more concise meaning can be gained using the principle of *'first mention.'* According to Biblical hermeneutics (the science of interpreting ancient text), when an important word or concept occurs for the first time in the Bible, the context in which it is used sets the pattern for its primary usage and development all throughout the Scriptures. The first time righteousness is mentioned in the Bible was when Abraham *believed* in God, based on the *vision* He received from Him.

"Look now toward heaven, and count the stars if you are able to number them." And He said to him, "So shall your descendants be." And he [Abraham] believed in the Lord, and He accounted it to him for righteousness.
- Genesis 15:5-6

Righteousness, in its simplest form, is the state of being in divine agreement with God. More specifically, embracing the revelation of your divine identity! Although Abraham had no heir, he believed in the God-given vision of being the *'father of many nations,'* and this was counted onto him as righteousness. From that point onward, Abraham's *self-image* underwent a profound transformation, in accordance with the vision bestowed upon him by God. In many instances, a divine revelation serves the ultimate purpose of unveiling your true self - guiding you along a trajectory where you are intricately linked with the people, resources, and opportunities necessary for fulfilling your purpose and embodying whom God designed you to be.

Therefore, what makes mammon 'unrighteous,' particularly when amassed in substantial amounts, is because it is a means of obtaining almost anything you want, void of **discovering your true self**. Righteousness, on the other hand, empowers you to manifest the good that you desire from the position of your **Divine Identity**.

Individuals who believe they can obtain anything through financial means often fall into the trap of placing their faith in money and the pursuit of material possessions. However, as we will explore later in this book, this pattern serves as yet another instance of leading a life void of understanding your true self.

BUY WITHOUT MONEY

The righteous manifest the good they desire through an understanding of who God created them to be. While many believe that their desires can only be fulfilled with money, those who understand righteousness **buy without money!**

Everyone who thirsts, come to the waters; and you who have no money, come, buy and eat. Yes, come, buy wine and milk without money and without price.
- Isaiah 55:1

HOW CAN ONE BUY WITHOUT MONEY?

On the surface, this may seem absurd; however, buying without money is a powerful spiritual principle that every living person on the planet can deploy! Moreover, as I will explain later in this book, buying without money is integral to the *gospel of Christ*. The good news of a spiritual Kingdom of unlimited resources and power, by which one can obtain the good that they desire *if they believe*.

SERVING TWO MASTERS

Despite the fact we are to buy without money, Jesus tells us to be *faithful* with the unrighteous mammon, and God keeps *providing* ways for us to have more of it in our pockets! No wonder there is so much ambivalence on the subject of God and money! To address this issue and hopefully resolve the *perceived* conflict between God and money, let us carefully examine Jesus' statement regarding God and mammon.

"No one can serve two masters; for either he will hate the one and love the other, or else he will be loyal to the one and despise the other. You cannot serve God and mammon."

- Luke 16:13

At first glance, it looks like Jesus is saying,

> **"Money is the enemy and God's biggest rival."**

> **"You cannot serve two masters, so you must choose between God and money."**

> **"Your antipathy for money is proof of your love and devotion to God."**

> "Those who desire to be rich,
> have taken their side against God."
>
> "Your choice in this matter
> will determine your eternal destiny!"

This is the sentiment of many who believe that money is the *root* of all evil!

ALTHOUGH, MONEY IS OFTEN USED TO CIRCUMVENT THE NEED FOR GOD, DOES THAT MEAN WE CANNOT HAVE BOTH GOD AND MONEY?

First of all, money *is not* the root of all evil. Only the *love* of it is *(1 Timothy 6:10)*. Second, Jesus did not say you cannot *'have'* God and mammon, He said you cannot *'serve'* God and mammon. This is a very important distinction. Money is a resource and a tool, nothing more, nothing less! It is not something you should either love or hate! If you pay attention to what Jesus is saying you will understand that when it comes to God and money, *loving one and hating the other*, or *being loyal to one and despising the other* is the consequence of serving two masters! The person whose love for God is *defined* by their *hatred* towards money *(and those who have it)* is in the same boat as the person whose love for money defines their animosity towards God. Knowingly or not, **both are serving two masters!**

To be clear, I am not saying you should not have any convictions in regard to riches gained by greed, corruption, or unlawful practices. What I am saying is,

> "If your love or hatred towards money
> defines your relationship with God,
> you are serving two masters."

God vs Money

The perceived conflict between God and money is as preposterous as a confrontation between the reigning heavyweight boxing champion of the world and an ant! Such a contest would be dismissed as utterly inconceivable. However, envision a scenario where this unlikely duel is arranged, and substantial wagers are placed on the ant emerging victorious. To even entertain such a notion, one would need to perceive the ant as astonishingly magnified or the boxing champion as drastically diminished. As illogical as this idea might sound, it pales in comparison to the absurdity of likening God to money. Although God has no equal, whatever you compare to God is either deified or magnified!

•

God does not want you to love or hate money.

•

God wants you to be trustworthy enough to have plenty of money for your own benefit and the benefit of others.

•

You can have as much money as you need or desire as long as money does not have you!

•

Money will either be your hardworking slave or your brutal master. It is in your power to determine which it will be.

"Every gold piece you save is a slave to work for you.
Every copper it earns is its child that can also earn for you."

"You do eat the children of your savings,
then how do you expect them to work for you?
And how can they have children that will also work for you?"

- George S. Clason's book, The Richest Man in Babylon.

CHAPTER 2
CHRIST V CHRISTIANITY

"You have the poor with you always, and whenever you wish you may do them good; but Me you do not have always"

There was certainly no ambiguity amongst those who penned the Bible *(under the inspiration of the Holy Spirit)* whether one should be rich or not. The standard of living encouraged requires one to have at least *seven* streams of income.

Ship your grain across the sea; after many days you may receive a return. Invest in seven ventures, yes, in eight; you do not know what disaster may come upon the land.
- *Ecclesiastes 11:1-2 NIV*

> **YOU MUST BE AS SERIOUS ABOUT GETTING WEALTH AS GOD WAS IN EMPOWERING YOU TO HAVE IT.**

Living life abundantly is the gold standard of godly living. To this end, having multiple streams of income is not merely a luxury; it is a necessity. Most millionaires became wealthy by having multiple streams of income. By focusing on accumulating wealth in this manner, you avoid the unpredictable cycle of 'get rich quick' schemes. This approach requires time, patience, meticulous planning, and, naturally, prayer—embodying the spiritual qualities essential for successful living. **GOD WANTS YOU TO BE RICH AND WEALTHY!** Never again to be broke or in financial bondage! To achieve that aim, He has given you the power to get wealth.

*"And you shall remember the Lord your God, **for it is He who gives you power to get wealth,** that He may **establish His covenant** which He swore to your fathers, as it is this day."*
- *Deuteronomy 8:18*

God made a covenant for you to get wealth. A covenant is the most binding contract one can enter into, and breaking it has grave consequences. Therefore, you must be as serious about getting wealth as God was in empowering you to have it. Not only that, but once you have gained wealth, you must make it clear to everyone that **God made you rich!**

Hence, there's no need to feel ashamed of your affluence. When it comes to being wealthy, there are just two significant errors you can commit:

1. Thinking you made yourself rich.
Both riches and honour come from You, And You reign over all. In Your hand is power and might; In Your hand it is to make great and to give strength to all. (1 Chronicles 29:12)

2. Putting your trust in your riches.
He who trusts in his riches will fall, but the righteous will flourish like the green leaf. (Proverbs 11:28 NIV)

If you are rich, and you recognize God as your provider, then you should let everybody know that *it was Him*, that gave you the power to get wealth. Take note of what God states in Deuteronomy 8:18,

"**When** *you have eaten and are full.*"
"**When** *you have built beautiful houses and dwell in them.*"
"**When** *your silver and your gold has multiplied.*"
"**When** *all that you have is multiplied.*"

God does not have a problem with you having far more than you need!

This smacks in the face of those who believe it is ungodly for believers to have excess or abundance. Not only that but God wants you to thrive and not just survive. Therefore, elevate your aspirations to thriving, beyond mere survival. While one house could suffice for survival, inhabiting beautiful homes might be what you need to truly flourish. While a single job might meet survival needs, cultivating multiple streams of income is what you need to thrive. God wants to supply your need according to *His* riches in glory, rather than by your low self-worth.

DIVINE EXTRAVAGANCE

Thriving is the standard of living God desires for His children. It is His will for you to live not just abundantly but *exceedingly abundantly*.

Now to Him who is able to do exceedingly abundantly above all that we ask or think, according to the power that works in us, to Him be glory in the church by Christ Jesus to all generations, forever and ever. Amen.

Ephesians 3:20-21

This could will be interpreted as **divine extravagance,** the type of extravagance that God does not equate to waste! Indeed, godliness, humility and divine extravagance go hand in hand. This may not sit comfortably with many Christians, nevertheless, the Bible attests to that fact that God embodies extravagance!

Extravagant in living...

He has cattle on a thousand hills (Psalms 50:10)

He has a house with many mansions (John 14:2)

The walls of His city are made of jasper and garnished with all manner of precious stones (Revelations 21:19)

The streets in heaven are made with gold so pure, it looks like clear glass (Revelations 21:21)

And in giving...

He does exceedingly and abundantly above what we ask or think. (Ephesians 3:20)

He pours out blessings from heaven that we cannot contain. (Malachi 3:10)

He satisfies us abundantly with the fatness of His house and causes us to drink from the river of His pleasures. (Psalms 36:8)

He gave King Solomon what he did not ask for - riches and honor like no other. (1 Kings 3:13)

That being said,

"IS IT WASTEFUL FOR A CHRISTIAN TO HAVE, FOR THEIR OWN PERSONAL USE, SOMETHING THAT IS EXTRAVAGANT OR VERY EXPENSIVE IN PRICE?"

As long as the quality matches the price tag or it is being put to good use, should it really matter? Consider Christ's response to being anointed with a fragrance oil worth more than three times the average yearly wage!

And being in Bethany at the house of Simon the leper, as He sat at the table, a woman [Mary Magdalene] came having an alabaster flask of very costly oil of spikenard. Then she broke the flask and poured it on His head. But there were some who were indignant among themselves, and said, **"Why was this fragrant oil wasted?** *For it might have been* *sold for more than three hundred denarii and **given to the poor.**"* And they criticized her sharply. ***But Jesus said,** "**Let her alone.** Why do you trouble her? **She has done a good work for Me.** For you have the poor with you always, **and whenever you wish you may do them good;** but Me you do not have always. She has done what she could. She has come beforehand to anoint My body for burial.*

- Matthew 14:3-8

Spikenard is a plant that only grows in the Himalayan mountains of India and Nepal. The fragrant oil derived from this plant was a rare, imported product in Israel, hence the hefty price tag. According to the disciples, the flask of spikenard oil held an estimated value of over 300 denarii. A denarius represents a day's wage for a common laborer. Using the average day's pay of $175 for a laborer in the USA, the value of the oil poured onto Jesus' head would be approximately $52,500 in today's economy.

The disciples' reaction to what Mary had done was one of indignation. Indignation is a feeling of righteous anger, arising from witnessing, performing, or hearing something considered morally wrong. Jesus' disciples were indignant because, from their point of view, pouring such an expensive oil on *His* head appeared wasteful. They justified their anger, arguing that,

> 'THE OIL COULD HAVE BEEN SOLD FOR A GREAT PRICE, AND THE MONEY GIVEN TO THE POOR.'

This sentiment has stood as a rallying point against any 'believer' owning anything extravagant, be it a luxury sports car, a boat, or even a plane. This stance remains unchanged, regardless of how much they have already given to those in need.

"HOWEVER, WHAT IS REALLY BEING IMPLIED HERE?"

Putting aside the fact that it was Mary's prerogative to do what she wants with her expensive luxury item - if the oil should be sold and the proceeds given to the poor, **then someone has to buy it.** That being the case,

"IS THE BUYER MORE DESERVING OF THE EXPENSIVE LUXURY ITEM THAN CHRIST?"

"MOREOVER, IS THE BUYER MORE DESERVING OF THE EXPENSIVE LUXURY ITEM THAN YOU?"

In this present time, the expensive luxury item could be a:

- Clive Christian Sandalwood perfume ($8000)
- Hublot Swiss Watch ($43,000)
- Louis Vuitton crocodile-skin handbag ($55,500)
- Lamborghini Huracán ($300,000)
- Khalilah superyacht ($33M)
- Gulfstream G700 private jet ($75M)

Or any other high-end luxury product.

If as a Christian, you are uncomfortable with believers enjoying such luxuries, you may well feel such items should be sold and the money given to the poor. After-all, *that would be the Christian thing to do.* Don't get me wrong, I whole-heartedly believe that everyone should aspire to become a **philanthropic giver.** I applaud those who, out of their abundance, have generously given away cars and houses to help those in need. However, such actions should be undertaken joyfully and out of love, rather than due to external pressure, misplaced criticism, or feeling coerced into guilt due to one's wealth. Jesus' response to all this, is far removed from a typical Christian response. First of all, He silences the critics of the woman's actions, making it clear that her deeds are not wasteful but *commendable*, and should therefore be left alone! He then goes on to say,

> *"You have the poor with you always,*
> *and whenever you wish you may do them good;*
> *but Me you do not have always."*

What a profound statement! How would you respond if any prominent minister or pastor, criticized for their wealth, offered the same retort? [selah] At first glance, Jesus' statement might appear heartless and self-centered, yet upon closer contemplation, this is not the case.

The disciple's indignation at the oil being wasted, implies 2 things:

1. Jesus is not worthy to be anointed with so expensive an oil.
2. A perception that there is lack and insufficiency.

In contrast, Jesus' response stems from the fact that:

1. He is worth infinitely more than any item of great price.
In addition, *you too* are infinitely more valuable than any expensive luxury item, having been made in the image of God. As such, expensive luxury items are for *your* enjoyment when it is in your means to do so.

2. In the Kingdom of Heaven, there is no such thing as lack and insufficiency. A believer can make a *withdrawal* whenever they wish for the benefit of those in need, as well as for themselves.

Jesus exemplified the essence of the Kingdom when He fed more than 5000 people from just five loaves and two fish *(Matthew 14:15-21)*. He replicated this extraordinary provision when He fed more than 4000 people from just seven loaves and a few fish *(Matthew 15:32-39)*. Both of these remarkable events transpired in remote and barren places. These examples are but a glimpse into the multitude of miraculous *'works'* He undertook to demonstrate the Kingdom. His entire earthly ministry was dedicated to exhibiting the fundamental truth that:

'There is a spiritual dimension of unlimited resources and power available to all who would believe. This is the Kingdom of God, which is in you. It's power and resources can be manifested in your life, and in the lives of others, through the faith of the Son of God.'

This is the gospel of the Kingdom. The gospel that Jesus preached! This is the gospel His disciples witnessed *'up close and personal'* in the three years they spent under His tutelage. Not only did they witness the feeding of the multitudes, they were also the ones handing out the food!

They were there when Jesus turned water into wine.
(John 2:1-11)

They were there when a colossal haul of fish was caught. This was done, at Jesus' command, after they had spent the whole night fishing without any success. *(Luke 5:1-11)*

They were there when Jesus commanded Peter to go to the lake, open the mouth of the first fish he caught, take the coins he will find in there, and pay the temple tax for them both. *(Matthew 17:27)*

> **GODLINESS, HUMILITY AND EXTRAVAGANCE GO HAND IN HAND.**

And…

They all knew that Jesus was the Christ, the Son of the living God.
(Matthew 16:16)

Given all that they knew and witnessed firsthand,

"WHY WOULD THEY CONSIDER THE POURING OF EXPENSIVE OIL ON JESUS' HEAD TO BE A WASTE AND MORALLY WRONG?"

Also…

"WHY WOULD THEY EVEN SUGGEST SELLING THE OIL TO FEED THE POOR, HAVING WITNESSED THE UNLIMITED POWER AND RESOURCES OF THE KINGDOM?"

No matter how expensive the oil was, this line of thinking not only contradicts the gospel of the Kingdom, but is also an *insult* to Christ! Anyone who criticizes and disparages a believer because of their wealth is essentially insulting 'The One' through whom such wealth came. To be in Christ, is to be 'at one' with God. What belongs to Him, belongs to *you*.

That being said, I do not believe the disciples *knowingly* insulted Christ in the way they did. As a matter-of-fact, I don't believe any Christian knowingly insult Christ, as they do, when they criticize their fellow brothers and sisters because of their wealth! It's surprising, though, considering the disciples' understanding of Christ, that they responded with such indignation toward the woman's use of the oil.

"SO, WHERE DID THE NOTION OF THE OIL BEING WASTED REALLY COME FROM?"

The answer can be found when you read John's account of this event:

Then Mary took a pound of very costly oil of spikenard, anointed the feet of Jesus, and wiped His feet with her hair. And the house was filled with the fragrance of the oil. Then one of His disciples, Judas Iscariot, Simon's son, who would betray Him, said,

"Why was this fragrant oil not sold for three hundred denarii and given to the poor?" This he said, **not that he cared for the poor, but because he was a thief,** *and had the money box; and he used to take what was put in it. - John 12:3-6*

Judas was the instigator and catalyst for the disciple's misplaced indignation! He was the one who insinuated that the expensive oil was being *wasted* on Jesus. Due to his trusted position as the treasurer (keeper of the money box), his words carried a lot of weight; causing the other disciples to align with *his* line of thinking. However, while the disciples' reaction emerged from a moral standpoint, Judas' remarks were motivated by immoral intentions. Judas was a thief! He regularly pilfered money from the money box, which must have had a considerable amount of money, as none of the other disciples detected any discrepancies. Adding to the gravity of the situation is the revelation that he was under the direct influence of Satan. This is evident from the Bible's account that Satan entered Judas on the eve of Christ's betrayal.

Now the Feast of Unleavened Bread drew near, which is called Passover. And the chief priests and the scribes sought how they might kill Him, for they feared the people. **Then Satan entered Judas,** *surnamed*

Iscariot, who was numbered among the twelve. So he went his way and conferred with the chief priests and captains, how he might betray Him to them.

- Luke 22:1-4

Although Judas was the ringleader, Satan was the one pulling the strings! Evidently, Judas had fallen under the sway of Satan's deceit for a considerable period, allowing Satan to seize the opportunity to enter him without resistance. This illustrates how open Judas was to Satan's way of thinking. Satan, known as the father of lies and the accuser of the brethren, utilized the blueprint that underlies all his stratagems in the accusation against Mary:

- **An ungodly agenda - Cloaked in morality**
- **Executed through blind zeal and righteous indignation.**

DON'T BE DECEIVED

We must, therefore, be aware of the perniciousness of Satan, who is adept at polluting minds and tainting perspectives. He achieves this by planting the seeds of his ideology into the collective consciousness, extending even to the realm of the church. This is the same strategy he used on Eve when he tempted her to eat the forbidden fruit.

Now the serpent was more cunning than any beast of the field which the Lord God had made. And he said to the woman, "Has God indeed said, 'You shall not eat of every tree of the garden?'" And the woman said to the serpent,

"We may eat the fruit of the trees of the garden; but of the fruit of the tree which is in the midst of the garden, God has said, 'You shall not eat

it, nor shall you touch it, lest you die.'

"Then the serpent said to the woman, "You will not surely die. For God knows that in the day you eat of it your eyes will be opened, and you will be like God, knowing good and evil."
- *Genesis 3:1-5*

First of all, God did not say they will die if they *touched* the fruit! He only said they will die if they *eat* the fruit. As Adam was the one God gave this command to, he may have been the one who *added* this extra stipulation as a preventative measure for Eve. Nevertheless, it was a deviation that could easily be exploited. Imagine what went through Eve's mind when she reached out and touched the fruit and *did not die*. Straight away it would seem that the serpent was telling the truth! This then made it easier for her to proceed with disobeying God's command.

Secondly, Eve was tempted by the suggestion that she could be like God if she ate the fruit. However, since *she was already like God*, having been created in His likeness, it appears she was deceived into believing she could be more than she already was. Even the slightest deviation from God's word can lead us into bondage, affecting our relationships, health, career, and finances. This, combined with a lack of understanding of our true identity, has wrought immeasurable devastation upon the world, impacting all of our lives in one way or another.

As the title of this chapter implies, there is a disparity between Christ and many aspects of Christianity due to a deviation from the word of God and ignorance of our divine identity. This observation is not meant to offend but to shed light on the state of many Christians in relation to Christ. A crucial aspect of this disparity is the perception of

Jesus. This is vitally important because the core tenet of the Christian faith is for believers to be like Christ, conforming to His image.

*For whom He foreknew, He also predestined to be **conformed to the image of His Son**, that He might be the firstborn among many brethren.*

- Romans 8:29

To be conformed to the image of Christ is to embrace His thinking, character, and **self-image**. You cannot conform to the image of the Son of God with a distorted perception of Him. Nowhere is the image of Christ more impaired than in the perception of Him being *poor*.

Many Christians' attitudes towards wealth, spirituality, identity, and life as a whole stem from this misconception. However, this misunderstanding impacts not only the church but also the world. Christian values, shaped by how Christ is perceived, exert varying degrees of influence over all of us. Many of these values contribute to advancing society and humanity on a larger scale. Nevertheless, within these values lies an insidious concept that has negatively affected numerous cultures and societies—the so-called *'Virtue of poverty.'*

Over the centuries, the virtue of poverty has created a domino effect, obstructing the financial well-being, aspirations, potential, and even the health of countless well-meaning individuals caught in its far-reaching tentacles. Although only a relatively small fraction of people formally vow to embrace poverty, the belief that poverty holds virtue—implying that wealth is inherently ungodly—has cast a long shadow over the thoughts, education, and choices of billions of industrious individuals around the world.

A not too distant relative of the virtue of poverty is the belief that one should not strive to be rich but *comfortable*. Although being comfortable means different things to different people, it generally means being able to:

- **Pay for your all bills and living expenses**
- **Pay off any debt (or keep up on loans and credit card payments)**
- **Drive a new car**
- **Go on holidays**
- **Put money away for a rainy day**
- **Improve the overall quality of your life.**

Although on the surface this may seem quite reasonable, it is one of the most selfish ambitions one could have! Especially if you are a Christian! This is certainly not the thinking of our heavenly Father, who desires to:

- **Pour out for you such blessing that there will not be room enough to receive it,**
- **Lavishly satisfy you with the fullness of His house and cause you to drink from the rivers of His pleasures,**
- **Do exceedingly and abundantly above all that you ask or think,**

And so much more.

All for the purpose of you being a *blessing* to your community, and to the nations. We all have a responsibility to *'be more'* so that we can *'have more'* and *'do more'* to improve the lives of others. God's model for living is for our *'cup to run over,'* so that from the overflow of abundance, we can make a significant difference in the world.

CHAPTER 3

THE PROFILE OF GOD'S LEADING SERVANTS

◆

"Let the LORD be magnified, who has pleasure in the prosperity of His servant"

God takes pleasure in the prosperity of His servant - a sentiment consistently illustrated throughout the Bible. When examining the lives of the most prolific of God's servants, you will find they were no stranger to wealth and riches. As a matter of fact, by today's standards, they were super-rich!

ABRAHAM'S WEALTH

The concept of 'wealth' is first introduced in the Bible through the life of Abraham. In Genesis 13, we learn that he possessed an abundance of livestock, along with significant holdings of silver and gold. Additionally, he commanded his own private army. Even his nephew Lot, who journeyed with him, possessed considerable livestock. Their collective possessions were so great that the land could not accommodate them both!

ISAAC'S WEALTH

Abraham's son, Isaac, lived in the land of the Philistines and became a very prosperous man. Genesis 26 tells us that he grew rich and prospered more and more until he became very wealthy, to the point where the Philistines envied him. Eventually, Abimelech, the King of the Philistines, told him to depart from the land because he had become too powerful.

JACOB'S WEALTH

Despite Jacob's reputation as a trickster, both by name and by deed, he was exceedingly blessed. He was extraordinarily skilled in raising and tending to sheep and cattle, displaying remarkable proficiency. His father-in-law, Laban, amassed significant wealth simply by having Jacob in his employ. When the time came for Jacob to branch out from under Laban with his growing family, the Bible says he increased exceedingly, acquiring much cattle, maidservants, menservants, camels, and asses *(Genesis 30:43)*.

JOB'S WEALTH

Apart from Jesus, Job stands as one of only two men in the Bible described as blameless or perfect in their walk with God. He was the greatest man in the East, boasting an impressive inventory of wealth. This included seven thousand sheep, three thousand camels, five hundred yokes of oxen, five hundred female donkeys, and an enormous household. By a conservative estimate, Job's net worth in livestock before his tribulation would amount to over $28 million in today's economy. However, after enduring his trials and losing everything except his wife, the Lord *blessed his latter days more than his beginning*, giving him twice the number of livestock he had before, elevating his net worth to approximately $56 million in today's economy.

JOSEPH'S WEALTH

Although Joseph was born into a wealthy family, his story is one of rags to riches, having been sold into slavery by his own brothers. Even in the role of a slave, the Bible describes him as a "prosperous man" solely because the Lord was with him *(Genesis 39:2)*. Joseph also had the divine gift of interpreting dreams, a spiritual gift that played a pivotal role in his ascent to prominence.

Despite being falsely accused of attempted rape and subsequently imprisoned, his gift ultimately brought him before the King of Egypt. Through his interpretation of the King's dream, Joseph emerged as the second most powerful figure in a nation that, during that era, was the wealthiest and most advanced in the known world.

ELISHA'S WEALTH

Elisha was the protégé and eventual successor of the prophet Elijah. Although little is known about his life before meeting Elijah, the significant number of oxen he was plowing with when he encountered Elijah suggests he came from a wealthy land-owning family (1 Kings 19:19). He was undoubtedly the most prolific of the Old Testament prophets, having inherited a double portion of Elijah's spirit. Unlike his predecessor, who led a solitary existence, Elisha frequently engaged with the kings of Israel and was a homeowner, despite his ministry taking him far and wide.

While Elisha declined the generous "blessing" offered by Naaman, which consisted of:

- 10 talents of silver,
- 6,000 pieces of gold,
- 10 changes of raiment,

(which in today's economy would have run into millions of dollars),

there is no indication that he turned down the gift from the King of Syria, which comprised 60 camels laden with "every good thing of Damascus." The camels alone would be valued at nearly a million dollars by today's standards, and in accordance with ancient customs, the contents they carried would amount to several millions more.

DANIEL'S WEALTH

Daniel's story closely mirrors that of Joseph. He, too, was born into privilege and nobility but was subjected to servitude, in this case within Babylon. Just as Joseph possessed the divine gift of dream interpretation, so did Daniel, a skill pivotal to his ascent to prominence. His interpretation of King Nebuchadnezzar's dream, which confounded Babylon's wise men, led to his receiving many *'great gifts.'* Daniel was also made ruler over the whole province of Babylon and chief governor of all the wise men in Babylon (Daniel 2:48). By now, it should be evident that in the ancient world, a 'gift' from a king or someone of great influence usually amounted to several million dollars in today's economy.

So, affluence was pretty much commonplace for God's leading servants. They most likely would have been ranked amongst the elite echelons of today's super-rich. Be this as it may, their wealth and riches amounted to *'pocket-change'* compared to the personal fortunes and vast revenues of the Kings of Israel. In particular, David and Solomon.

DAVID'S WEALTH

King David's wealth was so substantial that as he neared the end of his life, he left behind a legacy for his son, Solomon, providing the necessary resources for the construction of the temple.

Indeed, I have taken much trouble to prepare for the house of the Lord one hundred thousand talents of gold and one million talents of silver, and bronze and iron beyond measure, for it is so abundant. I have prepared timber and stone also, and you may add to them.

- 1 Chronicles 22:14

The standard unit of weight for trading gold and silver in today's economy is the troy ounce. To put it in perspective, 100,000 talents of gold corresponds to approximately 96,452,239.71 troy ounces. Considering that gold's current value hovers around $2,300 per troy ounce (as of the time of this writing), David's contribution in gold tallies up to an astonishing sum of over $221.8 billion. His silver donation (based on the current price of $23 per troy ounce) amounts to over $24.4 billion today. And let's not forget the bronze and iron, which were too innumerable to measure! This substantial contribution toward the construction of God's temple only represents a fraction of David's wealth. Much of his fortune stemmed from the spoils of his numerous military triumphs. He also received tribute from entities like the Moabites and potentially other neighboring nations.

SOLOMON'S WEALTH

Although, King Solomon inherited the considerable wealth amassed by his father, God still bestowed upon him an even greater abundance of riches. In fact, Solomon's wealth surpassed that of any other king who came before him and those that came after!

Solomon went up there to the bronze altar before the Lord, which was at the tabernacle of meeting, and offered a thousand burnt offerings on it.

On that night, God appeared to Solomon, and said to him, "Ask! What shall I give you?"

And Solomon said to God: "You have shown great mercy to David my father, and have made me king in his place. Now, O Lord God, let Your promise to David my father be established, for You have made me king over a people like the dust of the earth in multitude. Now give me wisdom and knowledge, that I may go out and come in before this people; for who can judge this great people of Yours?"

And God said to Solomon: "Because this was in your heart, and you have not asked riches or wealth or honour or the life of your enemies, nor have you asked long life - but have asked wisdom and knowledge for yourself, that you may judge My people over whom I have made you king - wisdom and knowledge are granted to you; and I will give you riches and wealth and honour, such as none of the kings have had who were before you, nor shall any after you have the like."

- 2 Chronicles 1:6-12

A significant portion of this wealth materialized in the form of gifts presented by various dignitaries and heads of state who journeyed from all corners of the world to seek Solomon's wisdom. Among these visitors was the Queen of Sheba, who was so impressed with Solomon's wisdom and opulence that she gave him "One hundred and twenty talents of gold, spices in great abundance, and precious stones" *(2 Chronicles 9:9)*. The value of the gold alone translates to $333 million in today's economy.

Other revenues came thanks to his large shipping fleet and his partnership with the King of Tyre. Through this partnership, he acquired a great deal of gold, silver and ivory, along with an assortment of exotic commodities. In addition to offerings from merchants and Arabian monarchs, he received an annual tribute amounting to six hundred and sixty-six talents of gold from the territories under his dominion. This annual tribute alone equates to over $1.8 Billion in today's economy.

Solomon's wealth was thus a fusion of gifts, trade partnerships, tribute payments, and the bounty of his own flourishing kingdom.

To reiterate, wealth and affluence were commonplace among God's leading servants, as well as those who walked in His ways. However, none of these great men of God are characterized primarily by their riches.

- **Abraham is celebrated as 'the father of faith.'**

- **Isaac symbolizes 'God's promise,' embodying the miraculous birth arising from 'hope against hope.'**

- **Jacob, subsequently named Israel, was known as the one who has 'struggled with God and with men and prevailed.'**

Indeed, the privilege bestowed upon these three patriarchs is evident when God introduces Himself as "The God of Abraham, Isaac, and Jacob." Thus, their names are forever intertwined with God's identity, signifying their profound significance in the divine narrative.

- **Elisha is remembered as a revolutionary prophet who inherited a double portion of Elijah's spirit.**

- **Job is known for his unshakeable faith in God, even in the face of overwhelming afflictions.**

- **Joseph and Daniel stand out as exceptional interpreters of visions and dreams, guiding their respective kingdoms through their insights.**

- **Daniel was also known for his outstanding faith, highlighted by his willingness to face death in the lion's den.**

- **David is known for being the 'worshipping warrior.' The only man to be described as 'being after God's own heart.'**

- **Solomon's renown lies in his unparalleled wisdom, making him the wisest man to have ever lived**

All were fabulously rich, yet their righteousness, acts of faith, and unwavering devotion to God far outshone the riches they possessed. Importantly, their wealth did not hinder their relationship with God; on the contrary, it was an outpouring of His goodness and blessing, stemming directly from their deep relationship with Him. These blessings manifested as divine gifts and power, making many of them invaluable assets to their nation.

The wealth of God's leading servants was woven into the broader tapestry of their lives, contributing to their ability to fulfill God's purposes and play significant roles in His unfolding plan.

CHAPTER 4
THE GRACE OF OUR LORD JESUS

"For you know the grace of our Lord Jesus Christ, that though He was rich, yet for your sakes He became poor"

C harles Spurgeon's assertion that it is *'Anti-Christian and unholy for any Christian to live with the object of accumulating wealth'* was part of a sermon he preached in 1867, entitled: 'Our Lord's Involuntary Poverty.' The thinking behind this sermon is based on how the following scripture is often interpreted:

The Grace of Our Lord Jesus

For you know the grace of our Lord Jesus Christ, that though He was rich, yet for your sakes He became poor, that you through His poverty might become rich.

- 2 Corinthians 8:9

It is widely believed that the above text is *clear proof* that Christ was only rich in His *preincarnate*, heavenly existence. But, for our sakes, relinquished His *celestial abundance* to live a life of destitution, being born to an impoverished carpenter and his wife. Charles Spurgeon goes onto say,

"There was no period of the Savior's life on earth in which it could be said that He was rich, but He became poor. It must, therefore, have been in a previous state of being that our Lord was rich—and I shall now ask your thoughts to go back to the time when Jesus Christ was rich. Poor are our words!"

That being the case, we should *follow Jesus' example* and seek only to be rich *spiritually* while being poor *materially*. According to Spurgeon, those who follow the example of Christ in this way are considered to be *'Advanced Christians.'* He goes on to applaud the likes of John Wesley, who died in poverty leaving but *'two spoons,'* having served God with all that he had.

I whole-heartedly agree that we should follow Jesus' example. As a-matter-of-fact it is imperative that we do! However, as I will show you later in this book, the widely held belief that Jesus was poor in this life, is **TOTALLY UNTRUE**.

When we consider the fact that:

1. **Poverty is a curse** *(Genesis 3:17-19)*
2. **Christ only became a curse on the cross** *(Galatians 3:13)*
3. **Therefore, any exchange from being rich to becoming poor could only have took place on the cross** *(2 Corinthians 5:21)*

...then the Apostle Paul's statement regarding *'the grace of our Lord Jesus Christ,'* is *clear proof* that Jesus was indeed rich in this life, and not just in heaven! Therefore, the example we must follow is:

'Being rich like Jesus'

We must follow the Lord's example of having immense wealth but not allowing that wealth to have mastery over our lives.

Even if we were to consider the notion that Christ's wealth exists solely in heaven, and we should indeed entertain this idea, how can we reconcile this belief with the assertion that *"As He is, so are we in this world"* *(1 John 4:17)*? The Bible states, **"As He is"** (present tense), not *'As He was.'* Jesus currently resides in heaven, where, by worldly standards, He is undeniably and profoundly rich beyond imagination. Given this reality, regardless of which side of the fence you reside, the example we are called to emulate is:

'Being rich like Jesus'

That is the grace of our Lord Jesus. The reason He became poor *on the cross*.

CHAPTER 5
CONFRONTING THE VIRTUES OF POVERTY

◆

"It is more blessed to give than to receive"

Although God's leading servants often possessed wealth, a prevailing notion persists that it is more *'godly'* to be poor. Many regard wealth as a potential obstacle to faith and view affluence as inherently sinful. This belief endures despite numerous instances in the Bible where God blesses His children with material wealth. From generation to generation, Christians and non-Christians alike have been indoctrinated with this negative attitude towards wealth and riches.

Nevertheless, God has put eternity in the hearts of us all *(Ecclesiastes 3:11)*. Therefore, we are unlimited by nature, equipped with an instinctive desire to **"be more," "achieve more," "have more,"** and **"give more."** A poverty mindset stifles and confines your potential accomplishments, resulting in a life that fails to fully realize inherent potential and falls short of being who God created you to be.

Many of the perceived virtues associated with poverty have emerged from distorted and out-of-context interpretations of Christ's teachings, such as not serving 'God and mammon'—which I addressed in the first chapter. Another example is the misapplication of Jesus' counsel to the 'rich young ruler,' urging him to *"sell all he possessed and follow Him."* This misinterpretation has formed a doctrine requiring all Christians to divest themselves of their earthly possessions, a perspective I will address later in this book.

It is important to recognize that being broke or poor does not inherently draw you more closer to Christ than being rich does. On the contrary, 'lack' can prove to be even more distracting than material wealth, especially if your thoughts are consumed by the concerns of meeting your daily needs.

Being wealthy no more equates to being materialistic than being poor equates to godliness. As repeatedly demonstrated by the faith heroes of the Bible, a life of faith is determined by your relationship with God, which can be enjoyed whether one is rich or poor.

Nevertheless, a considerable number of devout men and women, driven by their deep religious convictions, feel a sense of obligation to take a vow of poverty and relinquish all their worldly possessions. Their motivation lies in dedicating their lives to God and assisting the poor and destitute. While the intent behind taking a vow of poverty to aid the impoverished is commendable,

> **"IS THIS APPROACH REALLY THE MOST EFFECTIVE WAY TO HELP THE POOR, OR INDEED, HUMANITY AS A WHOLE?"**

Here are some reasons why this question must be asked:

WE ARE CALLED TO BE AGENTS OF CHANGE

The gospel of the Kingdom is supposed to be *'good news'* to the poor. To someone living in poverty, good news would be the realization that they are not bound to remain in a state of destitution. However, it's noteworthy that many religious orders, feel it necessary to *be poor* in order to *help the poor!* Their intention is often to provide solace to the poor, or in some cases *champion* the cause of the poor. But where is the impetus to change one's circumstances so that they are no longer poor? Indeed, how effective can you be in transforming the lives of the poor when your beliefs hinge on the virtues of poverty? You certainly will do nothing to change a person's life from poverty to prosperity! The very thing God wants above everything else *(3 John 1:2).*

If a vow is to be taken, let it be a commitment to become an **agent of change**, guiding lives from the clutches of darkness into the radiant embrace of God's marvelous light. The dichotomy between darkness and light is a constant concept, whether it pertains to good and evil, foolishness and wisdom, sickness or health, or rich or poor. When we permit God to work through us to influence someone's life, the difference between their previous situation and their current state should be like night and day.

WE ARE CALLED TO DO MORE GOOD

In his book, 'Business Secrets from The Bible,' Rabbi Daniel Lapin, widely known as 'America's Rabbi,' makes a startling comparison between the venerable Mother Teresa and MicroSoft founder, Bill Gates. He asks the question, **"Who out of the two did 'more good' for more people?"** This question is asked on the premise that,'**He who helps more people is doing more good than he who only helps a few.**'

Mother Teresa is well-deserving of praise for her tireless work in caring for thousands or even hundreds of thousands of poor people in Calcutta. However, Microsoft products have improved the lives of hundreds of millions of people worldwide.

Therefore, as hard as it may be for some to hear, Bill Gates *(amongst others Billionaires)* has done more good for mankind than Mother Teresa - and that can be measured quantitively. Here is another notable point Rabbi Lapin makes:

"Wealth is God's way of incentivizing you to do exactly what He wants you to do, which is to care obsessively about satisfying the needs and desires of His other children. Cynics may denounce 'monetary motivation' as greed but this is false thinking. The virtue of service is in no way compromised or diminished by the monetary reward for doing so."

– Rabbi Daniel Lapin

So few people sing Bill Gates' praises alongside Mother Teresa because they have adopted the mistaken view that *benefitting* from the good one does somehow *diminishes* the virtue of that good deed. However, this is a 'Win-Win' because doing good for others and earning a living from it is a self-perpetuating model of universal success.

WE ARE CALLED TO BE GIVERS

If there is a virtue to be found in being poor, it is when scarcity places a greater demand for wealth to flow into your life. The saying, *"Necessity is the mother of invention,"* is not said without merit, and to quote American businessman and philanthropist, Jon Huntsman Sr,

> **"When facing severe challenges your mind is normally at its sharpest."**

George Müller, a Prussian Christian Evangelist, resided in Bristol, England during the 19th Century. Operating solely through the power of prayer, this great man of faith established an impressive network of orphanages that accommodated more than 2,000 children at a time. Astoundingly, Müller achieved this monumental feat without possessing any personal wealth of his own. His mission was rooted in the aspiration to rescue vulnerable orphans who would otherwise have been consigned to perilous workhouses or the harsh realities of the streets. His driving force was to offer them not only care, but also education and training.

Yet, paramount to Müller's endeavors was his profound desire to manifest the visible evidence of a living God who responds to prayer. To this end, he garnered approximately £1.4 million in donations (equivalent to £32.5 million in today's economy) over the course of his lifetime. Remarkably, he acquired this without asking anybody but God for a single penny. Stories abound of God's divine providence. One breakfast time there was no food. Müller confidently said grace. Immediately there was a knock at the door. It was the local baker who had woken in the night with a feeling that God was telling him the orphans had no bread. So at 2.00am, he got up and baked some for them. Shortly after this came another knock at the door, the milkman's wagon had broken down outside the orphanage. He asked if he could give them his milk, so as to be able to empty and repair his wagon. There was also another time when a young woman from a very wealthy family donated almost three quarters of a million dollars in jewels.

In addition to acknowledging George Müller's steadfast faith, it's crucial to recognize the pivotal role that wealthy individuals played in fulfilling what was requested through prayer. As Müller adhered to a principle of never personally seeking financial assistance from others, the considerable donations and substantial sums of money that flowed into his ministry could only have been facilitated by *God's hand* on those who had the means to give generously.

Often times, God uses wealthy people who are compassionate and giving, to answer the prayers of the poor in need. Take for example the good Samaritan who found a man robbed, beaten, and left for dead by the wayside. Not only did he have the compassion to stop and tend to his wounds, he also took him to an inn and paid the inn-keeper two denarii *(two days wages for a common laborer)* to take care of the man in his absence. He also promised to repay the inn-keeper whatever more was spent upon his return. The fact that he could make such a promise could only mean that the good Samaritan was a man of means.

Therefore, it is wrong to joyfully receive donations from wealthy people in one hand, while disparaging their wealth with the other. You will do well to remember that being able to give substantially to those in need is a key role of a believer. It is to a believer's credit to lend to others *without expecting anything back!* This can hardly be done by those who choose to live a life of poverty!

If you lend to those from whom you hope to receive back, what credit is that to you? For even sinners lend to sinners to receive as much back. But love your enemies, do good, and lend, hoping for nothing in return; and your reward will be great, and you will be sons of the Most High.

- Luke 6:34-35

THE WEALTH OF THE EARLY BELIEVERS

Finally, it's worth addressing the misconception that the vow of poverty assumed by various religious orders resembles true destitution. In reality, their lifestyle often deviates from the image of hardship that one might imagine. Consider, for instance, the St. Augustinians, a Christian order established in 1244. Their concept of communal poverty entails shared resources, where nothing is considered personal property. Members of this order live together in comfortable residences equipped with modern amenities like heating and air conditioning. They maintain a satisfactory diet, dress comfortably, and even drive well-maintained vehicles. Any funds acquired by an individual are pooled into a communal bank account, serving the collective needs of the members, and supporting the ministry's initiatives. This model is supposedly be modelled after the communal practices of the early Christian communities depicted in the book of Acts.

Now the multitude of those who believed were of one heart and one soul; neither did anyone say that any of the things he possessed was his own, but they had all things in common. And with great power the apostles gave witness to the resurrection of the Lord Jesus. And great grace was upon them all. Nor was there anyone among them who lacked; for all who were possessors of lands or houses sold them, and brought the proceeds of the things that were sold, and laid them at the apostles' feet; and they distributed to each as anyone had need.

- Acts 4:32-35

On the surface, the early believers' communal approach gives the impression that they lived devoid of any possessions, however, a closer examination reveals a different story. Their unity was so profound that individual ownership was inconsequential to them. In a display of solidarity, driven by the necessity to support one another amidst persecution and marginalization, those who owned lands or houses voluntarily sold them.

It's important to grasp that those believers who possessed land or property to sell could only have been the **wealthy landowners who converted to Christ.** It's equally significant to recognize that **they did not sell the homes they dwelled in!** For it was in *their* homes that the community of believers were able to break bread, fellowship, and praise God (Acts 2:46). This they did out of love and a common goal, not as a *prerequisite* for joining the faith.

To provide further clarity on this matter, let's delve into the case of Ananias and Sapphira, whose sudden demise resulted from their decision to withhold a portion of the proceeds from the sale of their land. Their fate struck fear in the hearts of those who heard of it.

But a certain man named Ananias, with Sapphira his wife, sold a possession. And he kept back part of the proceeds, his wife also being aware of it, and brought a certain part and laid it at the apostles' feet. But Peter said, "Ananias, why has Satan filled your heart to lie to the Holy Spirit and keep back part of the price of the land for yourself? While it remained, was it not your own? And after it was sold, was it not in your own control? Why have you conceived this thing in your heart? You have not lied to men but to God." Then Ananias, hearing these words, fell down and breathed his last. So great fear came upon all those who heard these things. And the young men arose and wrapped him up, carried him out, and buried him.

Now it was about three hours later when his wife came in, not knowing what had happened. And Peter answered her, "Tell me whether you sold the land for so much?" She said, "Yes, for so much." Then Peter said to her, "How is it that you have agreed together to test the Spirit of the Lord? Look, the feet of those who have buried your husband are at the door, and they will carry you out." Then immediately she fell down at his feet and breathed her last. And the young men came in and found her dead, and carrying her out, buried her by her husband. So great fear came upon all the church and upon all who heard these things.

- Acts 5: 1-11

Ananias and Sapphira sold a piece of land they possessed *(not their home)* but withheld some of the proceeds from the sale. The questions is,

WERE THEY REQUIRED TO GIVE 'ALL' THE PROCEEDS OF THE PIECE OF LAND THEY SOLD?

Not at all! In his condemnation, Peter said it was *their choice* whether to sell the land or not, and after they sold it, it was *their choice* as to how much of the proceeds they wanted to give.

IN THAT CASE, WHY DID THEY DIE?

They died because they wanted to make out that they were giving *all* of the proceeds of the land they sold. The only reason for this is because they wanted to be perceieved as *righteous*. Much like the Pharisees and Sadducees, their concern was fixated on the external semblance of righteousness, rather than having a clean heart. They mirrored what Jesus referred to as, *"Whitewashed tombs which indeed appear beautiful outwardly, but inside are full of dead men's bones and all uncleanness."* (Matthew 23:27)

The motivation of the early church believers did not revolve around *self-imposed poverty,* nor was it a requirement. Their focus was not on practicing communal poverty, but rather **communal wealth.** Many of them willingly exchanged personal affluence for **shared abundance.** This was only done to ensure that **none in their midst would experience lack or need.** Therefore, it's crucial to understand that the intent of the early believers was not to *endorse* poverty; but to **eradicate it!**

- **Poverty is not a virtue.**
- **Poverty is a curse.**
- **Poverty is not godly.**
- **God wants poverty eliminated.**

The communal wealth model proved to be the most pragmatic approach for the early believers to eradicate any form of scarcity or necessity within their community, specifically addressing financial needs. As demonstrated by the Augustinians, any collective or religious order that patterns its way of life after the early believers will inevitably find themselves in a more advantageous position compared to those who struggle to make ends meet.

It's crucial not to fall into the misconception that living without earthly possessions is the epitome of godliness. It's highly doubtful that the wealthy land-owning believers would have sold land and properties if none among the church were facing lack or necessity.

Remember, it is not God's will for you to live with lack in any aspect of your life. This is precisely why God has pledged to personally meet all your needs.

> **My God shall supply all your need according to His riches in glory by Christ Jesus.**
>
> - Philippians 4:19 -

CHAPTER 6
BORN INTO WEALTH

◆

She wrapped Him in swaddling clothes, and laid Him in a manger, because there was no room for them in the inn...

Scholars and teachers alike have often said that Joseph and Mary were poor. They argue that as a carpenter, Joseph would have belonged to the lowest echelons of society—too poor to own farmland, uneducated, and forced to live off whatever carpentry or manual labor he could find.

Born Into Wealth

Further assumptions of Joseph and Mary's *supposed* poverty are drawn from the account of their journey to the Jerusalem temple to dedicate Jesus to the Lord.

Now when the days of her purification according to the law of Moses were completed, they brought Him to Jerusalem to present Him to the Lord (as it is written in the law of the Lord, "Every male who opens the womb shall be called holy to the Lord"), and to offer a sacrifice according to what is said in the law of the Lord, **"A pair of turtledoves or two young pigeons."**

- Luke 2:22-24

The requirement for the firstborn male to be presented to the Lord in such a manner can be found in the book of Leviticus, where many such rituals and sacrifices are detailed. In all versions of the Bible except the King James Version, the offering of a pair of turtledoves or two young pigeons is construed as a provision made by Moses for those who couldn't *afford* to offer what was originally required – that being a lamb. Consequently, a pair of turtledoves or two young pigeons is deemed as the *poor person's sacrifice.*

When the days of her purification for a son or daughter are over, she is to bring to the priest at the entrance to the tent of meeting a year-old lamb for a burnt offering and a young pigeon or a dove for a sin offering. He shall offer them before the LORD to make atonement for her, and then she will be ceremonially clean from her flow of blood.

These are the regulations for the woman who gives birth to a boy or a girl. **But if she cannot afford a lamb, she is to bring two doves or two young pigeons,** *one for a burnt offering and the other for a sin offering. In this way the priest will make atonement for her, and she will be clean.*

- Leviticus 12:6-8 (NIV)

While these factors may initially suggest that Joseph and Mary were poor, a more in-depth examination reveals a different narrative.

To begin, let's address the assertion that Joseph's occupation as a carpenter would have placed him among the poorest of the poor. To assess this claim, we need to delve into the societal framework of Judaean culture.

THE HAVE'S AND THE HAVE NOTS

To date, the only source of information on Judaean society in ancient times is the Bible. Despite ongoing archaeological excavations, no substantial supplementary material has been unearthed on this topic. Even the scant epigraphical sources discovered in Palestine have not significantly contributed to our understanding of this domain. Writers of the time only incidentally touched upon grassroots aspects of society and social issues. As a result, the Bible indirectly offers a glimpse into the social structure and customs of that distant era.

From this limited vantage point, we've discerned that there was a considerable gap between the rich and the poor, with a relatively slender middle class, *if any*. Consequently, ancient Judaean society primarily comprised two groups: 'The Haves' and 'The Have Nots.' 'The Haves' owned the land, and 'The Have Nots' worked the land. Numerous instances of wealthy landowners are found in the Bible, including figures like Abraham, Isaac, and Jacob. Wealthy landowners are also featured in some of Jesus' parables.

Those who worked the land are also mentioned in Jesus' parables, such as sowers, farmers, and hired hands.

Within Judaean society, those who fell into the category of extreme poverty were often subjected to mistreatment and were regarded as social outcasts. This ostracism was primarily rooted in the theological concept of *'reward and punishment,'* wherein compliance with God's commandments resulted in prosperity and well-being, while disobedience led to poverty and adversity. However, James vehemently rebuked the hostility directed toward the poor, especially when such discrimination took place within the confines of the church.

My brethren, do not hold the faith of our Lord Jesus Christ, the Lord of glory, with partiality. For if there should come into your assembly a man with gold rings, in fine apparel, and there should also come in a poor man in filthy clothes, and you pay attention to the one wearing the fine clothes and say to him, "You sit here in a good place," and say to the poor man, "You stand there," or, **"Sit here at my footstool,"** *have you not shown partiality among yourselves, and become judges with evil thoughts?*

- James 2:1-4

In conjunction with the wealthy landowning class, the societal landscape also encompassed a spectrum of roles including merchants, officials within the royal court, religious leaders, governmental administrators, esteemed fishing lineages, and skilled *artisans*. Among these artisans were individuals with invaluable craftsmanship abilities, such as engravers, embroiderers, goldsmiths, stonecutters, and most notably, ***carpenters***. Most of the Pharisees came from middle-class artisans, such as the apostle Paul who was a tentmaker. In addition, artisans played a vital role in spiritual life, as their expertise was relied upon for the critical task of building the tabernacle, the temple, and the ark of the covenant.

Then the Lord spoke to Moses, saying:

"See, I have called by name Bezalel the son of Uri, the son of Hur, of the tribe of Judah. And I have filled him with the Spirit of God, in wisdom, in understanding, in knowledge, and in all manner of workmanship, to design artistic works, to work in gold, in silver, in bronze, in cutting jewels for setting, in carving wood, and to work in all manner of workmanship.

*And I, indeed I, have appointed with him Aholiab the son of Ahisamach, of the tribe of Dan; and **I have put wisdom in the hearts of all who are gifted artisans, that they may make all that I have commanded you:** the tabernacle of meeting, the ark of the Testimony and the mercy seat that is on it, and all the furniture of the tabernacle - the table and its utensils, the pure gold lampstand with all its utensils, the altar of incense, the altar of burnt offering with all its utensils, and the laver and its base - the garments of ministry, the holy garments for Aaron the priest and the garments of his sons, to minister as priests, and the anointing oil and sweet incense for the holy place. According to all that I have commanded you they shall do."*

- Exodus 31:1-11

As a carpenter, Joseph was in **high demand** for his services, and as a result, he was a man of considerable means. Which makes perfect sense because, in a world whose *infrastructure* was primarily made of **wood,** how could he not be!! Carpenters of ancient times played pivotal roles in the construction of ships, chariots, cities, and palaces complete with their intricate furnishings and fixtures. Therefore, the notion of Joseph being amongst the poorest of the poor and having to survive hand-to-mouth by whatever carpentry work he could get is ridiculous at best!

ONLY THE RICH PAID TAXES

Further evidence of Joseph's wealth is embedded in the story behind Jesus' birth. First of all, as a descendant of David, Joseph was required to travel from Nazareth to Bethlehem, his ancestral home, *(where David was born)*, to register for the tax census.

And it came to pass in those days that a decree went out from Caesar Augustus that all the world should be registered. This census first took place while Quirinius was governing Syria. So all went to be registered, everyone to his own city. Joseph also went up from Galilee, out of the city of Nazareth, into Judea, to the city of David, which is called Bethlehem, because he was of the house and lineage of David, to be registered with Mary, his betrothed wife, who was with child.

- Luke 2:1-5

This required him to officially record his name, income, and any property he possessed in the public records. If, indeed, Joseph and Mary were the poorest of the poor, with no income or land, why would they have to register for tax? Only those who had a substantial income and property need register for tax.

ONLY THE RICH COULD AFFORD TO TRAVEL LONG DISTANCES

Secondly, in ancient times, embarking on long journeys when and wherever one likes is a luxury the poor could not afford. When Joseph and Mary left their home in Nazareth to register for the census registration in Bethlehem, they were faced with a daunting 90 mile expedition. This would have been an arduous journey, traveling south along the flatbeds of the Jordan River, then venturing west over the hills surrounding Jerusalem, and on into Bethlehem. This was no small feat, especially as Mary was heavily pregnant at the time. The journey would have taken almost two weeks and would require them to travel on horses, mules or donkeys, and have plenty of provisions if they were to survive such a grueling journey. Anyone who could make such a trip would most likely hire a guide or travel in a caravan of other travelers such as merchants or with friends and relatives for protection against bandits. As all of these options required great financial expense, this was not a journey a poor person was able to make.

We must understand that biblical writers were often *laconic* about certain events because it was always assumed that specific details would be common knowledge to the people of that time. So, the nativity story we see depicted during Christmas is far removed from the historical reality! From what is revealed later in the book of Luke, traveling in a caravan of relatives and friends was the most likely option Mary and Joseph took. We see the couple traveling in this manner when they brought Jesus to the temple when He was 12 years old.

Now his parents went to Jerusalem every year at the feast of the Passover. And when he was twelve years old, they went up to Jerusalem after the custom of the feast. And when they had fulfilled the days, as they returned, the child Jesus tarried behind in Jerusalem; and Joseph and his mother knew not of it.

But they, supposing him to have been in the company, went a day's journey; and they sought him among their kinsfolk and acquaintance. And when they found him not, they turned back again to Jerusalem, seeking him. And it came to pass, that after three days they found him in the temple, sitting in the midst of the doctors, both hearing them, and asking them questions.

- Luke 2:41-46

So vast was their caravan that *an entire day* passed before they realized that the young Jesus was not among them! This mode of travel is more typical of a wealthy Bedouin family and is certainly not indicative of how a person of modest means would journey. In contemporary society, this could be likened to dignitaries or celebrities traveling with a large entourage.

Mary and Joseph traveled in this way every year to attend the feast of the Passover. Among the most significant religious observances in the Jewish calendar, the Passover holds a central place. The Jews celebrate the Passover *(Pesach in Hebrew)* in honor of the emancipation of the Children of Israel, who were guided out of Egypt under Moses' leadership. Given that Judaism marginalized the extremely impoverished from the core of religious activities, it appears unlikely that Joseph and Mary, would have embarked on such a voyage, had they been so poor.

THE POOR PERSON'S SACRIFICE

You may be asking,

"IF JOSEPH AND MARY WERE CLASSED AMONGST 'THE HAVES,' WHY DID THEY OFFER A POOR PERSON'S OFFERING DURING THE TIME OF JESUS' DEDICATION?"

The answer is simple - **they did not!** As mentioned earlier, all but the King James Version of the Bible state that the offering of *'a pair of turtle doves or two young pigeons'* was a provision made for those who could not afford a lamb (Leviticus 12:6-8). The King James Version offers us a more literal translation rather than an interpretation or

assumption of what is being said.
Instead of saying, **"If she cannot afford a lamb,"** it simply says,

"If she be not able to bring a lamb, then she shall bring two turtles, or two young pigeons..."

A more direct translation from Hebrew says,

"If her hand find not sufficiency of a lamb."

Which could simply mean: **If a lamb was not available.**

As a very specific lamb was required (a male lamb in its first year), it is very possible that such a lamb was not available to them at the specific time required. So at this point, it is not clear if a mother not being able to bring a lamb was due to *affordability* or *availability*. Fortunately, in another case where a sacrifice is required, the Bible *does* provide specific details of a **poor person's sacrifice.** This can be found in Leviticus 14, which gives us the sacrificial requirements for those seeking ceremonial purification from a skin disease. Here are the requirements listed in v.10,

- **Two he lambs without blemish**
- **One ewe lamb of the first year without blemish**
- **Three tenth deals of fine flour mingled with oil**
- **One log of oil**

After instructions are given in how the above list should be administered, in v.21, Moses then gives specific instruction for someone who is *'poor'* and not able to get all of the above items.

Here is the list of items for the **poor person's sacrifice:**

- One lamb
- one tenth deal of fine flour mingled with oil
- A log of oil
- Two turtledoves, or two young pigeons

Now let's remind ourselves of what was required for the dedication of a firstborn male: child:

– One male lamb in its first year,
or if her hand find not sufficiency for a lamb
– two turtledoves or two young pigeons.

As we can see from the list above, even a poor person should still be able to afford one lamb. Not only that, but a poor person should also have the means to provide two turtledoves or two young pigeons, **in addition to a lamb**. Therefore, what was mandated for the dedication of a firstborn male child—whether the mother was rich or poor — remained the same. That being the case, the issue of a mother not being able to bring a lamb has nothing to do with whether she could *afford* to or not! There must have been other factors as to why she was not able to obtain a lamb at that particular time. Factors that were probably not detailed because they were common knowledge to the people of that time.

We would do well to remember that all of the sacrifices and rituals in the old testamant was embodied by one person - that being Christ. Therefore, not only did Mary and Joseph present two turtledoves or two young pigeons, but they did indeed bring a lamb - *'The True Lamb'*—**Christ** in the flesh.

Much like Joseph, Daniel, and earlier prophets, Jesus was born into wealth, not poverty. Joseph was a man of substantial means, renowned and esteemed in Judea—acknowledged not just as *'The Carpenter,'* but also as *'The Son of David.'* The Jewish populace awaited the arrival of the Messianic King, fully aware that he would hail from the lineage of David. Consequently, any descendant of David would inherently hold a position of nobility, irrespective of how many generations had passed.

The humble circumstances of Jesus' birth were solely due to the overcapacity in Bethlehem on that particular day, resulting in there being *'no room at the inn.'* This implies that Mary and Joseph initially attempted to *pay* for accommodation but were met with a full house. However, by the time the Magi made their appearance, Mary and Joseph had already acquired a house!

*When they saw the star, they rejoiced with exceedingly great joy. And when they had come into **the house**, they saw the young Child with Mary His mother, and fell down and worshiped Him.*

- Matthew 2:10-11

CHAPTER 7
A TRIBUTE FOR THE KING

*And when they had opened their treasures,
they presented unto him gifts...*

What is a fitting tribute for a King? More importantly, what tribute befits the *King of Kings?* A tribute is money or goods paid by kingdoms or nations to acknowledge the superiority of another kingdom. Apart from what was brought to him by merchants and Arabian Kings, Solomon received an annual tribute amounting to almost $2 Billion in today's economy.

Given this context and considering the customs of that time, where the value of a tribute given to a King or Queen reflects their eminence and significance, **should not Jesus receive much more?** After all, He is the King of a Kingdom far superior to any Kingdom of this world!

Thankfully, wise men, known as 'Magi,' took up the role of honoring Christ in this way. Unfortunately, various notions regarding these mysterious visitors from the East have obscured the enormity of their gifts. The traditional Christmas narrative would have us believe that the wise men's gifts to Jesus comprised of mere trinkets consisting of gold, frankincense, and myrrh. Some even say that the value of these gifts would have sufficed to fund the journey of Jesus, Mary, and Joseph to Egypt, a necessary escape from the threat of Herod. However, this portrayal can only be part of the many 'absurd traditions and conjectures' criticized by M.R. Vincent:

"Many absurd traditions and guesses respecting these visitors to our Lord's cradle have found their way into popular belief and into Christian art. They were said to be kings, and three in number; they were said to be representatives of the three families of Shem, Ham, and Japheth, and therefore one of them is pictured as an Ethiopian; their names are given as Caspar, Balthasar, and Melchior, and their three skulls, said to have been discovered in the twelfth century by Bishop Reinald of Cologne, are exhibited in a priceless casket in the great cathedral of that city."

- Vincent's Word Studies on the New Testament

Despite what you see on Christmas cards and nativity plays, we do not know how many wise men there were. Neither is there any mention of their names throughout scripture. The Bible only says, **"There came wise men from the East."** However, the fact that their entry into

Jerusalem sparked panic throughout the whole town indicates that there were far more than just three!

It's likely that the Magi's search for the "King of the Jews" was influenced by Daniel's impact on them during the Babylonian captivity. Daniel's significant role as their appointed master and his intervention that spared their lives must have left a profound impression. When King Nebuchadnezzar decreed the death of all Babylonian wise men for their inability to interpret his troubling dream, Daniel, after seeking the mercies of God, revealed and interpreted the dream. This act not only saved the lives of all the Magi but also enshrined Daniel in Magian and Babylonian history as Belteshazzar, master of the magicians *(Daniel 4:9)*.

Given Daniel's devotion to God, it's reasonable to assume he utilized his position to share his deep knowledge of God and the scriptures. Consequently, the Magi likely became acquainted with Jewish prophecies about the awaited Messiah, significantly shaping their search for the "King of the Jews."

SO, WHAT WAS THE VALUE OF THE TRIBUTE GIVEN BY THE MAGI?

Whilst the Bible does not provide an exact figure for the tribute offered by the Magi, delving into their background allows us to gain a better understanding of the potential scope of their offering. Fortunately, additional sources like the Book of Daniel and the writings of historians such as Herodotus contribute to illuminating the enigmatic lives and origins of these mysterious men from the East.

A Tribute for The King

THE MAGI

The Magi were a tribe of priests from the far East, entrusted with duties reminiscent of the priestly functions of the Hebrew tribe of Levi. Their activities encompassed a spectrum of endeavors, including medicine, astrology, and extensive research into natural phenomena. In addition to their scholarly pursuits, they were masters in the art sorcery and divination. Not surprisingly, the word "Magi" eventually evolved into "Magic," reflecting their deep association with the mystic arts.

Despite their pagan lineage, the Magi's practices and spiritual beliefs bore resemblance to Judaism in several aspects. For instance, they adhered to monotheism and conducted blood sacrifices. In addidtion, their use of bundles of miniature rods in ceremonies paralleled the Levitical priests' utilization of the Urim and Thummim for seeking divine guidance. Yet, the Magi's influence extended beyond spiritual realms, encompassing enormous political power. Holding esteemed positions within the Babylonian court, they retained their high standing even after the conquest of Babylon by the Medes and Persians, continuing their prominence within the Parthian Empire.

John MacArthur, a leading pastor, teacher, and author, sheds more light on the political power of the Magi in his Bible Commentary.

"No Persian was ever able to become king without mastering the scientific and religious discipline of the Magi and then being approved and crowned by them."

- The MacArthur New Testament Commentary

Indeed, the Book of Esther recounts the incident when Queen Vashti declined King Ahasuerus's summons to appear before him. Facing this challenge to his authority, the King consulted with the Magi for legal advice before rendering a decision regarding the situation.

"On the seventh day, when the heart of the King was merry with wine, he commanded Mehuman, Biztha, Harbona, Bigtha, Abagtha, Zethar, and Carcas, seven eunuchs who served in the presence of King Ahasuerus, to bring Queen Vashti before the King, wearing her royal crown, in order to show her beauty to the people and the officials, for she was beautiful to behold.

But Queen Vashti refused to come at the King's command brought by his eunuchs; therefore, the King was furious, and his anger burned within him.

*Then the King said to **the wise men who understood the times** (for this was the King's manner toward all **who knew law and justice**, those closest to him being Carshena, Shethar, Admatha, Tarshish, Meres, Marsena, and Memucan, the seven princes of Persia and Media, **who had access to the King's presence, and who ranked highest in the kingdom.**"*

- Esther 1:10-14

The law of the Medes and Persians was so solemn that it could never be repealed, *not even by the king*. This principle is evident in the 6th chapter of Daniel, where King Darius's officials deceived him into issuing a decree that irrevocably condemned Daniel to the lion's den. When the king realized the manipulation by his officials, he found himself powerless to overturn the decree he had unwittingly issued. This highlights the immense authority and finality associated with the law of the Medes and Persians.

Therefore, the fact that King Ahasuerus sought the counsel of the Magi on how to lawfully penalize Queen Vashti underscores their significant role within the judicial system and the core principles of the Medo-Persian governance. These details lend weight to the assertions made by certain historians that the laws of the Medes and Persians could indeed be attributed to the code of the Magi.

Given the level of power and influence the Magi wielded in the ancient Babylonian and Medo-Persian Empires, one can conclude that they are part of the fraternity that controlled the world in that era. As John MacArthur explains,

"Not only were the Magi responsible for making every monarch that was made in that era, they were also responsible for setting up the judges as well. They had a check system for the despotism that could grow out of a kingship, and so they were the judges that counter-balanced the dictator king."

The eastern empire of the Medes and Persians eventually evolved into the Parthian Empire, where the dominion of the Magi prevailed. This empire stood as the sole Kingdom that effectively withstood the sprawling Roman Empire. The numerous conflicts spanning from 53 BC to 217 AD between these rival empires bear an uncanny resemblance to contemporary geopolitical dynamics. When the Roman Empire expanded its boundaries to encompass Mesopotamia, the Parthian Empire had already established itself as a formidable and affluent force. The Parthian cities ranked among the largest globally, with robust trade routes extending into regions such as China.

The meeting point of Roman and Parthian domains stretched along the Mediterranean coastline, encompassing Syria, Jordan, and Palestine. At the juncture of Jesus' birth, the Parthians posed a significant threat

> **NOT ONLY WAS JESUS BORN INTO WEALTH, BUT BY THE TIME HE WAS TWO, HE WAS ALREADY A BILLIONAIRE!**

to the Romans and their aspirations for global supremacy. This tension reverberated in Israel, where the power struggle between the East and the West was palpable.

Imagine the profound impact of the Magi's arrival in Jerusalem. These influential kingmakers from the East, arriving in splendid regalia and oriental grandeur, likely accompanied by a substantial military contingent, galloping through the city on Persian steeds, demanding to meet the "King of the Jews." It is no wonder the whole of Jerusalem was in a panic at what initially looked like a Parthian invasion!

Clearly, the Magi's stature far surpasses how they are portrayed in nativity plays! They were priests, experts in divination, princes, supreme court judges, and kingmakers, whose influence and power remained intact throughout successive eastern empires.

With all that has been revealed about:

- The Magi's tremendous religious and political power,
- Their deep-seated interest in the prophesied Messiah,
- Plus the fact that in ancient times, a gift from a King or someone of great influence usually amounts to many millions in today's economy...

It is truly inconceivable to think that the Magi would embark on such a momentous journey to pay homage to Jesus, the King of Kings, with mere trinkets! Their entourage included not only their personal guards for protection but also individuals designated to transport the immense treasure they carried. This treasure was intended as a profound tribute to honor the divine King of the Jews.

*And when they had come into the house, they saw the young Child with Mary His mother, and fell down and worshiped Him. And when they had **opened their treasures**, they presented gifts to Him: gold, frankincense, and myrrh.*
- Matthew 2:11

To put it in modern-day vernacular, Jesus was *'Set for life!'* Not only was He born into wealth, but by the time He was two, **He was already a Billionaire!** While one might question the accuracy of such an assertion due to the Bible's silence on the precise value of the Magi's gifts, it's undeniable that Jesus was far from being poor. You need only look a little closer at His life to see the tell-tale signs of His immense wealth.

CHAPTER 8
JESUS YOUNG, GIFTED AND RICH

"If anyone says to you, 'Why are you doing this?'
say, 'The Lord has need of it'"

The perception of Christ being a poor righteous teacher and healer with *'nowhere to lay His head,'* stands in stark contrast to how He was regarded by the people of His time. Jesus was indeed rich, and the notion of Him being poor is an afront to His image! Well before He was seen as *'Messiah,'* those among whom He lived and walked amongst knew Him as a young man of royal lineage and substantial means. One only need study His life to see that He moved in the same circles of Israel's wealthy elite. He clearly knew many landowners, and His insight into their personal lives is reflected in the parables He told. However, apart from the miracles He did, Jesus was distinct from the wealthy elite in a critical way. He stood up for the poor and His message of liberation, empowerment, and prosperity was revolutionary. As previously mentioned, the poor were badly treated in Judaean society and were excluded from participating in the central worship of the temple. However, *'the poor'* was the focus of Jesus' message and mission.

"The Spirit of the Lord is upon me, because he has anointed me to preach the gospel to the poor..."

- Luke 4:18

"Blessed are you poor, for yours is the kingdom of God."

- Luke 6:20)

"Go and tell John the things you have seen and heard: that the blind see, the lame walk, the lepers are cleansed, the deaf hear, the dead are raised, the poor have the gospel preached to them."

- Luke 7:22

As a healer, Jesus ministered to those in need, addressing their physical, emotional, and financial ailments. Logically speaking, if you are sick, you wouldn't seek divine healing from someone suffering from health problems. Similarly, you wouldn't seek moral guidance from someone living immorally, or advice on prosperity from someone who is not prosperous themselves. Jesus had none of these shortcomings. His life and earthly ministry radiated perfect health, moral integrity, and prosperity.

There is no argument that Jesus lived a life free from sin and exemplified divine health. However, the fact that He was rich is not so obvious. This is mainly because, having been born into wealth and receiving a tribute that would see Him *'set for life,'* wealth and abundance were seamless parts of His life. Therefore, the writers of the four gospels placed no particular emphasis on His wealth, as it was largely taken for granted. Only the apostle Paul highlighted the fact that Jesus was rich. Not only that, but amid the myriad qualities that characterized Christ—such as the healings, miracles, sermons, His death, and resurrection—Paul links 'the grace of our Lord Jesus' with the fact that He was rich.

For you know the grace of our Lord Jesus Christ, that though He was rich, yet for your sake He became poor, so that you through His poverty might become rich.
- 2 Corinthians 8:9

Numerous scholars endeavor to interpret this by suggesting that Christ possessed wealth only in the heavenly realm, and then relinquished it when He dwelled on Earth. However, this assertion could not be further from the truth. As previously emphasized, the only occasion when Christ exchanged His virtues for humanity's burdens was upon the cross. Poverty, being among humanity's burdens, only became His in His crucifixion. Furthermore, the concept of wealth becomes obsolete in heaven, where insufficiency and lack are non-existent. Wealth is only relevant in contexts of scarcity. Hence, Jesus could have been wealthy solely during His time on Earth, and the atonement He facilitated for your prosperity can only be realized only in your lifetime.

Glimpses of Jesus' wealth can be seen through an understanding of the customs of ancient Judaean society. Therefore, in an attempt to restore Jesus' image, this chapter attempts to pull back the veil of customary differences between western eyes and ancient Jewish culture so we can see Jesus as everyone else did at that time. Let us begin at the event where Jesus' first miracle took place.

THE WEDDING AT CANA

On the third day, there was a wedding in Cana of Galilee, and the mother of Jesus was there. Now both Jesus and His disciples were invited to the wedding. And when they ran out of wine, the mother of Jesus said to Him, "They have no wine." Jesus said to her, "Woman, what does your concern have to do with Me? My hour has not yet come." His mother said to the servants, **"Whatever He says to you, do it."** *Now there were set there six waterpots of stone, according to the manner of purification of the Jews, containing twenty or thirty gallons apiece. Jesus said to them, "Fill the waterpots with water." And they filled them up to the brim. And He said to them, "Draw some out now, and take it to the master of the feast." And they took it.*

When the master of the feast had tasted the water that was made wine, and did not know where it came from (but the servants who had drawn the water knew), the master of the feast called the bridegroom. And he said to him, "Every man at the beginning sets out the good wine, and when the guests have well drunk, then the inferior. You have kept the good wine until now!" **This beginning of signs Jesus did in Cana of Galilee,** *and manifested His glory; and His disciples believed in Him.*

- John 2:1-11

In first-century Jewish culture, wedding feasts were held at the groom's home and were as grandiose as the budget of the house would allow. The six stone waterpots designated for purification and ritual cleansing indicates that this was a large home, as each vessel accommodated 20-30 gallons of water.

A wedding feast typically lasted for a week, and the host would have been obligated to provide lavish hospitality for the whole duration. Consequently, running out of wine would subject the host's family and the newlyweds to shame and ridicule. Mary was the first to raise concern about the dwindling wine, directing her son's attention to the matter. This might have been because the women's quarters were located near the wine's storage area, enabling her to identify the shortage before the men. Alternatively, it's plausible that the servants initially approached her with the issue, prompting her to inform Jesus. In either case, **as Jesus had not done any miracles up to that point, their sole reason for coming to Him was for Him to pay for a new supply of wine.**

While an entire village commonly congregated to celebrate a wedding, it was tradition for the attendees to assist in covering the associated costs. Given that Jesus and His disciples were *invitees*, it was not unusual for the servants to approach Him seeking financial support. Their appeal wouldn't have arisen had they not believed that **He possessed the means to contribute to the expenses.** It's worth noting that this transpired *before* Jesus had gained widespread recognition as the Messiah. This is evident from His words to *Mary, "My hour has not yet come,"* which signified that He had not yet commenced His official mission. Therefore, as an invited guest of this wealthy family, His presence at the wedding points to His social standing amongst the Jews.

JESUS HAD SOMEWHERE TO LAY HIS HEAD

One of the reasons why many preachers and scholars suppose that Christ was the poorest of the poor is because of the statement He made to one of His would-be followers:

"Foxes have holes and birds of the air have nests, but the Son of Man has nowhere to lay His head."

- Luke 9:58

"DID JESUS REALLY HAVE NOWHERE TO LAY HIS HEAD, OR WAS HE SPEAKING HYPOTHETICALLY?"

I believe the latter to be true. The Gospel of Matthew informs us that upon learning of John's imprisonment, Jesus departed from Nazareth and took up residence in Capernaum, a coastal town situated in the Zebulun region *(Matthew 4:12-13)*. Following this, two of John's disciples, Simon and Andrew, began to follow Jesus after their mentor proclaimed, *"Behold the Lamb of God!"* When they asked Jesus, *"Where He was staying?"* He responded with an invitation: ***"Come and see!"*** Not only did they see where He was staying, but they also *abode* with Him that day *(John 1:34-39)*.

Thus, it becomes evident that Jesus did indeed possess His own place — a place substantial enough to accommodate guests. This supports the notion that He had a place to lay His head.

For Simon and Andrew to ask Jesus where He was staying implies that He appeared to be a person who possessed his own residence rather than someone who was homeless. Beyond his renown as a teacher and healer, Jesus' wealth could have played a role in attracting certain 'would-be' followers. This notion is supported by the fact that Judas exploited his role as treasurer for personal gain. Furthermore, Jesus made it clear that not everyone who calls Him Lord shall enter into the Kingdom of heaven *(Matthew 7:21)*. Consequently, not all who chose to follow Jesus did so for genuine reasons. They were attracted to **'What He had'** instead of **'Who He was.'** A sentiment reflected by Jesus' candid appraisal:

"Truly, truly, I say to you, you are seeking me, not because you saw signs, but because you ate your fill of the loaves (John 6:26)."

Indeed, many of His disciples disappeared when the going got tough! Only eleven dedicated disciples stayed (Judas omitted) because of Who He was - 'The Christ, the Son of the living God' *(John 6:66-69)*.

Given Jesus' profound insight into the heart of man, it's plausible that His statement, *"Foxes have holes and birds of the air have nests, but the Son of Man has nowhere to lay His head,"* could have been a way of cautioning aspiring followers not to anticipate the ease and comfort they might have assumed would come with following Him.

Furthermore, Jesus' assertion that He had *"Nowhere to lay His head"* might also carry prophetic connotations, alluding to His impending crucifixion. Ultimately, it was on the cross that He found no reprieve for His head, as His body slumped downward, forcing a strenuous struggle to rise up on His nailed feet in a desperate bid to breathe. While the exact nature of this statement remains open to interpretation, what's certain is that **Jesus did indeed possess a place to rest His head—whether it was at His residence by the sea in Capernaum or at His family home in Nazareth.**

"THE LORD HAS NEED OF IT"

Another sign of Jesus' wealth is unveiled in His triumphant entry into Jerusalem. In preparation for this event, Jesus instructed two of His disciples as follows:

"Go into the village opposite you; and as soon as you have entered it you will find a colt tied, on which no one has sat. Loose it and bring it. And if anyone says to you, 'Why are you doing this?' say, 'The Lord has need of it,' and immediately he will send it here."
- Mark 11:2-3

To modern Western eyes, the significance of this event might not be immediately apparent. The disciples were essentially fetching a young donkey for Jesus to ride on. **"What's the big deal in that?"** one might ask. However, the attention the disciples received, especially from the men questioning why they were taking the colt, highlights that this was indeed *a very big deal!*

In order to grasp the significance of this ecvent, I want you to imagine being in London, and as you walked along the street, your gaze lands upon a Bentley. But this isn't just any Bentley – it's the Bentley State Limousine! Crafted for Her Majesty Queen Elizabeth II during her Golden Jubilee in 2002, this remarkable vehicle is the official state car. With only two in existence, each has an estimated value of $500,000. Even if you did not know it belonged to the Queen, its illuminated coat-of-arms and a pennant gracefully adorning the roof makes it clear that it belongs to royalty. You also know that there is no way you can approach such a car without attracting the attention of security! This is the same scenario the disciples were presented with.

In this bygone era, a colt was the mount of Kings, especially one that had never been ridden before! The colt, therefore, held the status of a State Limousine of that time and place. Possession of such a creature was a privilege reserved for royalty or those of immense prestige and affluence. To the people of that time, witnessing someone riding this colt would have been more significant than our contemporary experience of spotting a celebrity in a stretch limousine.

When Jesus was seen astride on that colt through the streets of Jerusalem, it is very likely that they took this as a sign that He intended to overturn the Romans and take His rightful place as their King.

According to the original Greek text, when Jesus told the disciple to say, *"The Lord has need of it,"* the underlying implication was that 'The Owner' had a requirement for the colt. The fact that the men *(likely employed to safeguard the colt)* readily accepted the disciples' explanation means that they found it entirely credible that JESUS was, indeed, the rightful possessor of the colt.

JESUS HAD FINANCIAL BACKERS

In addition to the tribute He received at birth, Jesus had financial backers! Much like Elisha and the prophets that preceded Him, Jesus received considerable gifts and monetary contributions from those He had healed.

And certain women, which had been healed of evil spirits and infirmities, Mary called Magdalene, out of whom went seven devils, and Joanna the wife of Chuza Herod's steward, and Susanna, and many others, which ministered unto him of their substance.

- Luke 8:2-3

It's worth emphasizing that Jesus neither relied on nor solicited financial assistance from anyone. As mentioned earlier, it was customary for those who possessed wealth to express their gratitude for divine healing by generously supporting the *man of God*. This is precisely what these women and others did when Jesus delivered them from their infirmities.

From what we can glean from the scriptures, it would appear these were wealthy women. Joanna, whose name meant *'Jehovah is a gracious giver,'* was the wife of Chuza. Chuza, whose name meant *'The Seer,'* served as the steward for King Herod Antipas, overseeing the management of his properties. Besides handling Herod's estates, Chuza, as the King's chief-of-staff, possessed keen insight and enjoyed the King's complete trust in all matters.

Hence, Joanna and her husband occupied a prominent position in Judaean society. While scant information exists about Susanna beyond her close association with Joanna, it's conceivable that she may have been one of 'the other women' who visited Jesus' tomb after His resurrection, alongside Joanna, Mary Magdalene, and Mary, the mother of James. Given Susanna's intimate connection to Joanna and the stark socioeconomic divides between *'The Haves'* and *'The Have nots,'* it's highly probable that Susanna held a position amongst the wealthy elite.

Among the women who supported Jesus, Mary Magdalene stands out as the most controversial. Despite being labeled a 'sinner' by the religious authorities of her time, her unwavering dedication to Jesus remained unparalleled. Not only did she anoint Jesus' head with precious spikenard oil *(equivalent to $52,500 in today's economy)*, but just four days earlier, she had similarly anointed His feet with the same exorbitant oil.

Then Jesus six days before the Passover came to Bethany, where Lazarus was which had been dead, whom he raised from the dead. There they made him a supper; and Martha served: but Lazarus was one of them that sat at the table with him. **Then took Mary a pound of ointment of spikenard, very costly, and anointed the feet of Jesus, and wiped his feet with her hair:** *and the house was filled with the odour of the ointment.*

- John 12:1-3

Undoubtedly, Mary emerges as a woman of substantial means who gave lavishly to Jesus. Judging from the tomb her brother, Lazarus, was buried in *(prior to being raised from the dead)*, a tomb very similar to the one owned by Joseph of Arimathea, Mary also belonged to a wealthy family. The close bond between Jesus and her family provides insight into the social strata within which He operated.

THE MONEY BAG

With all the financial backing Jesus received, coupled with His personal fortune, He had need of a treasurer! That role was bestowed upon Judas, who was entrusted with carrying Jesus' money bag. Unfortunately, Judas had a darker side and clandestinely helped himself to the contents of the bag *(John 12:6)*. The fact that he could embezzle from Jesus' funds for an extended period emphasizes the significant amount of money held within the bag.

"SO, HOW MUCH MONEY WAS IN THE BAG?"

Although the Bible never states how much money was in the bag at any given time, it's evident that Jesus wielded substantial *'spending power.'* On the eve of the Passover feast, the fateful night of Jesus' betrayal, Jesus said to Judas, *"What you do, do quickly."* As Judas held the money bag, the remaining disciples construed Jesus' statement as an instruction for him to buy what was needed for the forthcoming 'Feast of the Passover,' or to give something to the poor. For the other disciples to make that assumption implies that giving to the poor and providing for the disciple's needs was quite routine. Although not stated, it is very likely that family members might have accompanied the twelve disciples, and their financial needs would have also been met. This could well have been the case during the time Jesus had 72 disciples in His company!

When the disciples asked where they would eat the Passover meal, Mark 14 indicates that Jesus had already *booked* a large upper room at an inn, under the name, *'The Teacher.'*

Now on the first day of Unleavened Bread, when they killed the Passover lamb, His disciples said to Him, "Where do You want us to go and prepare, that You may eat the Passover?"

And He sent out two of His disciples and said to them, "Go into the city, and a man will meet you carrying a pitcher of water; follow him. Wherever he goes in, say to the master of the house, '

The Teacher says, "Where is the guest room in which I may eat the Passover with My disciples?" '

Then he will show you a large upper room, furnished and prepared; there make ready for us." So His disciples went out, and came into the city, and found it just as He had said to them; and they prepared the Passover.

- Mark 14:12-16

Jesus' day-to-day expenditure was high. However, whether He was catering to the needs of seventy-two disciples or the twelve, there was always a surplus in the money bag - money enough to buy food for well over 5000 people in one sitting!

When the day was now far spent, His disciples came to Him and said, "This is a deserted place, and already the hour is late. Send them away, that they may go into the surrounding country and villages and buy themselves bread; for they have nothing to eat." But He answered and said to them, "You give them something to eat." And they said to Him,

"Shall we go and buy two hundred denarii worth of bread and give them something to eat?"

- Mark 6:35-37

Although Jesus never told the disciples to *buy* something to eat, that is exactly what they thought He meant. Their query regarding whether they should buy 200 denarii worth of bread *(equivalent to $24,000 in today's economy)* wasn't meant as sarcasm, as some might speculate, but rather a genuine inquiry. In fact, the Wuest Expanded translation of the New Testament informs us that they had already started their journey before turning around to ask Jesus that question. So, although Jesus supernaturally fed the 5000 *(in addition to the women and children who were not counted in that number)*, it was well within His means to buy food for them all!

THEY DIVIDED UP HIS CLOTHES

In the account of Jesus' crucifixion, there's a revealing episode that underlines His wealth, where four soldiers competed for His clothes.

When the soldiers crucified Jesus, they took his clothes, dividing them into four shares, one for each of them, with the undergarment remaining. This garment was seamless, woven in one piece from top to bottom. **"Let's not tear it," they said to one another. "Let's decide by lot who will get it."** *This happened that the scripture might be fulfilled that said, "They divided my clothes among them and cast lots for my garment." So this is what the soldiers did.*

– John 19:23-24

It is doubtful that the Roman soldiers would have divided up Jesus' clothes if they were not anything of value. While it's true that Jesus did not adorn himself in the long, ornate robes favored by the Pharisees for ostentation, it doesn't negate the fact that His attire was of excellent quality.

Traditional Judaean dresswear comprised of an outer garment and undergarments. The simlāh, serving as the outer garment, was a sizeable rectangular piece made from coarse, heavy woolen fabric, though at times, it could be linen. This was pieced together with minimal stitching and featuring two openings for the arms. However, the Roman soldiers were not interested in the *form* of clothing Christ wore, just the material it was made of. That is why the garments were torn into four shares. As Roman clothing was commonly made of wool, Jesus' outer garment was likely made of the more expensive linen imported from Egypt. Only wealthy Romans could afford linen tunics, so the soldiers would have undoubtedly seized the opportunity to have linen tunics made using Jesus' attire.

The undergarment the soldiers drew lots for was also made from linen; however, this time, it was the *form* of clothing that was of greater value. Jesus' undergarment was a seamless garment woven in one piece from top to bottom. This seamless tunic would have taken remarkable skill and ingenuity to make, not something the average layperson could afford to buy. As Roman citizens wore tunics as an outer garment, this seamless tunic would have been quite a prize, giving a semblance of prestige and status when worn in Rome.

CONCLUSION

To the people whom Jesus lived amongst, it was no secret that He was rich! His social standing within Judaean society squarely places Him amongst *'The Haves,'* rather than the *'Have nots!'* Born into nobility as a son of David, He attended the weddings of wealthy landowning families and was often invited to dine in their homes. Unlike the very poor, who were excluded from the center of religious life, Jesus had unfettered access to the temple and synagogues from an early age, where He conversed with preeminent doctors and teachers of the law. Among other things, He owned a seafront house in Capernaum as well as a donkey and colt - the luxury cars of that era! Jesus lived life abundantly - the very life He wants us to live *(John 10:10)*.

In light of these realities, the very notion of Christ being amongst the poorest is unequivocally false. **Jesus was rich!** His birth was marked by the treasure trove He received from the mighty Magi, and His death saw Roman soldiers squabbling over His clothes!

Even Jesus' disciples became wealthy because of Him! For, what do you think they did with the great multitude of fish they caught at Jesus' command? A haul so astonishing that it strained the capacity of two ships, even causing them to start sinking (Luke 5:4-9). The answer is simple. They sold the fish and reaped the rewards! This outcome might shed light on why Simon Peter, overcome by the magnitude of this unexpected windfall, expressed feelings of unworthiness in the presence of such abundance. His words, *"Depart from me, for I am a sinful man,"* underscore his astonishment at the influx of wealth, which seemingly arrived without merit. After that life-changing event, they were all able to retire from the fishing business and follow Jesus!

No doubt, some of you will remind me that it was Christ Himself who said,

"It is easier for a camel to go through the eye of a needle than for a rich man to enter the kingdom of God."

However, as I will discuss later, the statements made against *'the rich'* throughout scripture have been grossly misconstrued as an endorsement to live a life void of earthly possessions. The so-called virtues of poverty go against **'the gospel of the Kingdom'** - the gospel that Jesus preached - of a heavenly dimension of unlimited power and resources, by which one can manifest the good that they desire, if only they believe.

BOOK 2
MIND BEFORE MATTER

PROLOGUE

THE MYSTERIES OF THE KINGDOM OF HEAVEN

To truly understand the teachings and the nature of the Bible, you must first understand the teachings and nature of Christ, as demonstrated in His earthly ministry.

In the beginning was the Word, and the Word was with God, and the Word was God. He was in the beginning with God. All things were made through Him, and without Him nothing was made that was made. In Him was life, and the life was the light of men.

- John 1:1-4

Jesus *is* the Word, the Word that was with God, and the Word **Who is God.** He is the Word that became *flesh* and dwelt amongst us *(John 1:14)*. The Bible also declares that He came in 'the volume of the book that is written of Him' *(Hebrews 10:7)*. Therefore, *every book* in the Bible points to Christ!

SO, WHAT IS IT THAT WE CAN LEARN ABOUT THE BIBLE FROM LOOKING AT JESUS?

Well, one of the most notable things about Jesus is that He often spoke in parables.

All these things Jesus spoke to the multitude in parables; and without a parable He did not speak to them, that it might be fulfilled which was spoken by the prophet, saying: **"I will open My mouth in parables; I will utter things kept secret from the foundation of the world."**

- Matthew 13:34-35

THE MYSTERY IN PARABLES

The Greek word for parable is *'Parabole,'* which means placing one thing by another's side. Parables present one story, with two meanings or versions, placed side by side. There is the *exoteric* - the literal, or *'outer'* meaning, and then there is the *esoteric* - the spiritual or *'inner'* meaning. The exoteric version or meaning is the one that is suitable to be imparted to **the crowd**. It is the meaning that is most *obvious* to the casual hearer. On the other hand, the esoteric is the true meaning, or what I like to call **'the power meaning.'** It is the meaning that is not so obvious, given to those with the mindset to *apply* Christ's teachings.

When Jesus spoke to the multitude, He spoke in parables, but when He was alone with His disciples, **He explained all things to them** *(Mark 4:34)*. Therefore, the outer meaning is for the *'spectator,'* or *'hearer of the word,'* whereas the inner or power meaning is for *'disciples,'* 'practitioners,' or *'doers of the word.'*

The purpose of the outer meaning is to help the practitioner *visualize* the dynamics of the inner version. Without the external analogy, the inner version may not make much sense. Therefore, both the outer and inner versions are essential for the practitioner or 'doer of the word.' The spectator, on the other hand, need only concern him or herself with the outer *(literal)* meaning. The book of James makes a clear distinction between *'hearers of the word'* and *'doers of the word,'*

Be doers of the Word, ***and not hearers only,*** *deceiving yourselves. For if anyone is a hearer of the Word and not a doer, he is like a man observing his* ***natural face*** *in a mirror; for he observes himself, goes away, and immediately forgets what kind of man he was. But he who looks into the perfect law of liberty and continues in it, and is not a forgetful hearer* ***but a doer of the work,*** *this one will be blessed in what he does.*
- James 1:22-25

Prologue: The Mysteries of the Kingdom of Heaven

YOUR DIVINE IDENTITY

Interestingly, the Greek word used in **'natural face'** is *'Genesis,'* which means source or origin. Therefore, the Word reflects your *original* self! The version of you, void of all negative labels and low self-worth. As God and His Word are one, your natural face *mirrored* in the Word, points to your divine identity. Jesus came to show you who you really are! That's why He wants you to not only *'hear the Word'* but also *'do the Word.'* This is the only way to embrace and function in your divine identity. To the one willing to embrace their divine identity, it is given to know **the mysteries of the Kingdom of heaven.**

And the disciples came and said to Him [Jesus], "Why do You speak to them in parables?" He answered and said to them, **"Because it has been given to you to know the mysteries of the Kingdom of heaven, but to them it has not been given."**
- Matthew 13:10-11

UNLOCKING THE MYSTERY

The true meaning of the Word is hidden from the crowd and casual observer but revealed to those who desire to practice what Christ preached. To practice what Jesus preached, you need to understand the mysteries of the Kingdom of heaven - **the secrets of your divine nature.** The keys to understanding these mysteries are *esoterically embedded* in many of the parables. However, there is one parable in particular that unravels the mysteries of all parables when understood correctly, and that is the parable of the sower.

But when He was alone, those around Him with the twelve asked Him about the parable [of the sower]... And He said to them, **"Do you not**

understand this parable? How then will you understand all the parables?

- Mark 4:10 and 13

When Jesus said, "All parables," we should not limit this to the parables told in the four Gospels but to the entire Bible! As mentioned, Jesus came in the **full volume of the book,** written of Him. As both the Old and New Testament Scriptures reflect the character and nature of Christ, His use of parables informs us that the entire Bible is a parable, made up of parables. Unlocking the Bible's mysteries reveals Christ, and a revelation of Christ is a revelation of your Ultimate Self.

SO, WHAT ARE THE KEYS EMBEDDED IN THIS PARABLE, BY WHICH WE CAN PERCEIVE THE BIBLE IN ITS TRUE LIGHT?

As mentioned, the outer version of a parable helps the practitioner visualize the dynamics of the inner meaning. So, let us begin with what was told to *the crowd*.

"Behold, a sower went out to sow. And as he sowed, some seed fell by the wayside; and the birds came and devoured them. Some fell on stony places, where they did not have much earth; and they immediately sprang up because they had no depth of earth. But when the sun was up they were scorched, and because they had no root they withered away. And some fell among thorns, and the thorns sprang up and choked them. But others fell on good ground and yielded a crop: some a hundredfold, some sixty, some thirty."

- Matthew 13:4-8

Now here is the esoteric or 'disciple's version' of the same parable:

Prologue: The Mysteries of the Kingdom of Heaven

"When anyone hears the Word of the Kingdom and does not understand it, then the wicked one comes and snatches away what was sown in his heart. This is he who received seed by the wayside.

But he who received the seed on stony places, this is he who hears the Word and immediately receives it with joy; yet he has no root in himself, but endures only for a while. For when tribulation or persecution arises because of the Word, immediately he stumbles.

Now he who received seed among the thorns is he who hears the Word, and the cares of this world and the deceitfulness of riches choke the Word, and he becomes unfruitful. But he who received seed on the good ground is he who hears the Word and understands it, who indeed bears fruit and produces: some a hundredfold, some sixty, some thirty."

- Matthew 13:19-23

The key elements in the parable of the sower are **the sower, the seed, the soil, and the fruit,** all of which are essential components for sowing and reaping. Many of the parables Jesus told involve these elements in various forms and permutations. Whether it be:

- **The Weeds Among the Wheat** *(Matthew 13:24-30)*
- **The Mustard Seed** *(Matthew 13:31-32)*
- **The Leaven** *(Matthew 13:33-34)*
- **Hidden Treasure** *(Matthew 13:44)*
- **Laborers in the Vineyard** *(Matthew 20:1-16)*
- **The Tenant Farmers** *(Matthew 21:33-45)*

All of these parables carry a sense of sowing and reaping. According to the disciple's version of the parable of the sower:

- The sower is God.
- The seed is God's thoughts.
- The soil is the heart (the subconscious mind).
- The fruit is the manifestation of thought sown in the heart.

THE POWER OF YOUR MIND

When thoughts are sown into the fertile soil of the subconscious mind, they have the potential to manifest into physical reality. The different types of soil or ground mentioned in the parable represent the varying conditions of the heart. Only *one* heart condition is conducive to bearing fruit, which is the mind that not only hears but also **understands, believes,** and *accepts* the Word as truth. Once a thought has been accepted as *truth* within the subconscious mind, it is only a matter of time before it materializes into physical reality. This is the divine law of the mind!

To the subconscious mind, there is no distinction between mental and physical actions. What you vividly imagine yourself doing or achieving is just as real within your mind as if you were physically engaged in those actions. What becomes real in your heart will eventually become real in your life. The only difference between a mental reality and the equivalent physical reality is 'time.' Therefore, what you truly believe in your mind should be taken more seriously than what transpires in your physical reality. That certainly was the perspective Jesus had as reflected in the following statement:

*"You have heard that it was said to those of old, 'You shall not commit adultery.' But I say to you that **whoever looks at a woman to lust for her has already committed adultery with her in his heart**"*

- Matthew 5:27-28

To the degree that you believe something to be true is the degree to which you will manifest that truth, whether it be "**a hundredfold, sixty, or thirtyfold.**" This underscores why Jesus often said, *"According to your faith, be it unto you."*

THE MYSTERIES OF THE KINGDOM PERTAIN TO THE MIND'S ABILITY TO MANIFEST THOUGHT.

HERE LIES THE SECRET OF YOUR DIVINE NATURE.

If this is the fundamental meaning behind the parable of the sower, then it follows that all parables, and indeed, all Scripture should be understood through the lens of the mind's ability to manifest God's thoughts. This understanding is crucial for being *"fruitful"* and for manifesting the Kingdom as Christ did.

God's first commandment to humanity was *"Be fruitful and multiply."* This commandment was not referring to procreation *(which came as the second command)* but instead, using your mind to manifest the good that you desire, and your mouth to *'Call those things that be not, as if they were' (Romans 4:17).* This is the means by which God's will is accomplished on Earth. Therefore, the principles, lessons, and promises found in the Bible should be seen in the context of how we manage our thoughts.

In essence, we are beings of thought endowed with the capability to manifest **God's thoughts.** God is good, and His thoughts are filled with goodness - thoughts of joy, peace, success, freedom, health, and prosperity. These thoughts are designed to prosper you, not to harm you, to provide you with a hope and a future *(Jeremiah 29:11).*

Jesus is the **true vine,** and we are the branches of the vine *(John 15:1-8).* The life of the vine flows into the branches, and as branches, we are expected to *express* the life of the vine as fruit. The life of the vine equates to God's thoughts, while the fruit represents the manifestation of His thoughts, expressed as the desired good that we bring into reality. Thus, Jesus declared:

"If you abide in Me, and My words abide in you, you will ask what you desire, and it shall be done for you. By this My Father is glorified, that you bear much fruit; so you will be My disciples."
- John 15:1-8

Therefore, our primary purpose is to manifest the good that we desire, not merely for our own benefit but also for the well-being of others.

You are only a disciple of Christ when you bear much fruit, that being, the goodness that stems from God's thoughts.

Your Heavenly Father is glorified when you bear much fruit.

If you are not manifesting God's goodness (success, joy, freedom, peace, prosperity, health, and wealth), you are neither fruitful nor a disciple of Christ!

It is God's good pleasure for you to have what you desire, through Christ's mind in you.
The creative power through which all things were made.

Overall, the teachings of Christ convey the profound principle that

'Mind comes before matter'

and materiality is the product of that which is spiritual. Therefore, the core of spirituality and prosperous living lies in the ability to manifest divine thought - the good that one desires.

CHAPTER 9
THE LESSON FOR THE RICH YOUNG RULER

PART ONE

"How hard it is for those who have riches to enter the kingdom of God"

If Jesus was so rich, why does Christianity portray Him as poor and destitute, with no where to lay His head? - One possible explanation is that, much like God's leading servants, Jesus' character, gifts, and qualities far surpassed His wealth.

The fact that He possessed riches was merely incidental, just as it should be for all those who embrace the good news of the Kingdom. However, the primary reason appears to hinge on how the story of the rich young ruler has been interpreted.

*Now as He was going out on the road, one came running, knelt before Him, and asked Him, "Good Teacher, **what shall I do that I may inherit eternal life?**" So Jesus said to him, "Why do you call Me good? No one is good but One, that is, God. You know the commandments: 'Do not commit adultery,' 'Do not murder,' 'Do not steal,' 'Do not bear false witness,' 'Do not defraud,' 'Honor your father and your mother.'*

"And he answered and said to Him, "Teacher, all these things I have kept from my youth." Then Jesus, looking at him, loved him, and said to him,

*"One thing you lack: **Go your way, sell whatever you have and give to the poor, and you will have treasure in heaven; and come, take up the cross, and follow Me."***

But he was sad at this word, and went away sorrowful, for he had great possessions. Then Jesus looked around and said to His disciples, "How hard it is for those who have riches to enter the kingdom of God!"

- Mark 10:17-22

Contrary to traditional beliefs, when Jesus instructed the young man to sell his possessions and give to the poor, He was addressing the young man's *unique* circumstances. It is not an instruction or doctrine that applies to all believers. It is crucial to make this distinction because many in the church base their views on:

- **The virtue of poverty**
- **The renunciation of material wealth**
- **The institutionalization of poverty in the priesthood**
- **and the view that those who do not practice poverty are void of Christ's Spirit,**

...rests upon Jesus' discourse with the rich young ruler.

The consensus amongst Christian commentators is that the story of the rich young ruler is a teaching on the detrimental impact that money and material wealth can have on one's pursuit of eternal life. Indeed, this young man sincerely sought righteousness and considered himself *faultless* regarding the law. However, being asked to sell all his possessions and follow Jesus was a price too high!

It is thus assumed that if the young man had loved God more than money, he would have been willing to sell what He had and follow Jesus. But because he was rich, he *clung* to his possessions and, as a result, *'lost out'* on eternal life. Based on this notion, Jesus aptly said,

"How hard it is for those who have riches to enter the kingdom of God! For it is easier for a camel to go through the eye of a needle than for a rich man to enter the kingdom of God."

Not only did Jesus masterfully demonstrate that this young man was *not* faultless in regard to the law, He also exposed the greed that lurked within his heart - the same greed that supposedly resides in all that are rich! Consequently, being affluent and having substantial possessions may hinder one from entering the Kingdom of God because there is a greater reluctance to relinquish these worldly attachments in order to follow Jesus.

However...

IS THIS REALLY WHAT THIS STORY IS ABOUT?

IS THE DETRIMENTAL EFFECT MONEY CAN HAVE ON ONE'S DESIRE FOR ETERNAL LIFE THE TRUE LESSON TO LEARN FROM JESUS' DISCOURSE WITH THE RICH YOUNG RULER?

DOES BEING RICH MEAN THAT YOU ARE GREEDY?

OR...

IS THERE A MORE PROFOUND LESSON TO BE LEARNED?

Before hastily criticizing and passing judgment on the rich young ruler, it's essential to consider these questions. If he was denied entry into the Kingdom for his reluctance to give up all his possessions, what fate awaits the multitude of Christians who fail to consistently give tithes and offerings? It would be overly simplistic to assume that only the wealthy would struggle to comply if the same directive to **"sell one's possessions and give to the poor"** were extended to all believers. In truth, the issue that the rich young ruler grappled with is one that all believers must confront to varying degrees, irrespective of their economic status.

IS GREED AND THE LOVE OF MONEY THE REAL ISSUE, OR IS IT SOMETHING ELSE?

It is indeed *'something else,'* and understanding the problem is key to unravelling why Jesus told the rich young ruler to sell what he had and give to the poor. To uncover the real issue, we must interpret

Jesus' instruction to the rich young ruler within the *context* of His broader teachings. Keeping this in mind, let us embark on our journey, starting with the occasion when Jesus cautioned His disciples to **beware of the leaven of the Pharisees and Sadducees.**

The Lesson for The Rich Young Ruler - Part 1

CHAPTER 10
BEWARE THE LEAVEN OF THE PHARISEES

---

*"You know how to discern the face of the sky,
but you cannot discern the signs of the times"*

Now when His disciples had come to the other side, they had forgotten to take bread. Then Jesus said to them, **"Take heed and beware of the leaven of the Pharisees and the Sadducees."** And they reasoned among themselves, saying, "It is because we have taken no bread." But Jesus, being aware of it, said to them, **"O you of little faith, why**

do you reason among yourselves because you have brought no bread? *Do you not yet understand, or remember the five loaves of the five thousand and how many baskets you took up? Nor the seven loaves of the four thousand and how many large baskets you took up? How is it you do not understand that **I did not speak to you concerning bread?** - but to beware of the leaven of the Pharisees and Sadducees."*

*Then they understood that He did not tell them to beware of the leaven of bread, but of **the doctrine** of the Pharisees and Sadducees.*

- Matthew 16:5-12

Moments before this event, Jesus rebuked the Pharisees and Sadducees for asking Him for a *sign* from heaven.

Then the Pharisees and Sadducees came, and testing Him asked that He would show them a sign from heaven. He answered and said to them, "When it is evening you say, 'It will be fair weather, for the sky is red;' and in the morning, 'It will be foul weather today, for the sky is red and threatening.' **Hypocrites!** *You know how to discern the face of the sky, but you cannot **discern** the signs of the times.*

- Matthew 16:1-3

Jesus called the religious leaders *'hypocrites,'* because they knew how to discern the face of the sky, but failed to *discern* the signs of the times. In other words, they knew how to recognize 'outward signs' that was *apparent* to all, but as Israel's Spiritual leaders, lacked the *spiritual discernment* required to understand the sign of the times.

Jesus calls those who rely on outward signs to guide their lives a **'wicked and adulterous generation.'** It was precisely for this reason that He cautioned His disciples to beware of the **doctrine** of Pharisees and Sadducees.

- **A doctrine based on the limitations of the outer physical world, rather than the infinite possibilities of your inner spiritual reality.**
- **A doctrine based on facts rather than truth.**
- **A doctrine that prides outward appearance over inner qualities.**

To explain this further, let me first present to you a basic illustration of reality.

INNER AND OUTER WORLD BASICS

In the Bible, the universe is described as the Heavens and the Earth. Heaven is the realm of God's mind, presence, and reality. It represents the *inner* spiritual world, whereas the earth represents the physical *outer* world. The outer world is the visible world rooted in an invisible world, that being spiritual. When we look at a plant, we know there is more to it than what we can see because its roots are hidden in the earth. This is a simple analogy of the universe: **the unseen spiritual realm coexisting with the visible physical world.**

When I use the term 'spiritual,' I'm not referring to any particular religion or faith but rather to that which is intangible yet undeniably real. For instance, thoughts are intangible yet profoundly real. Love, too, exists in the intangible realm but is immensely real. Even faith falls into this category—an intangible yet genuinely real force.

On the other end of the spectrum, fear and hate are intangible but very real. None of these aspects can be observed in their pure form in

> **THE INVISIBLE REALM IS THE REALM OF VISION**

the physical world; we can only perceive or experience their manifestations.

While the inner world remains invisible, it is, in essence, the realm of vision. The outer world, on the other hand, represents the manifestation of what is perceived in the inner world. *Hebrews 11:3* and *2 Corinthians 4:18* succinctly address this concept. When these two scriptures are put together, they provide profound insight into the true nature of our world.

> Through faith, we understand that the worlds were framed by the word of God, so that things which are seen were not made of things which do appear. While we look not at the things which are seen, but at the things which are not seen: for the things which are seen are temporal; but the things which are not seen are eternal.

Simply put;

- ***Things which are seen [tangible things] are made from things which are not seen [intangible things].***

Even science agrees that when matter is broken down to the *subatomic level*, all you are left with is energy.

- ***Tangible things are temporal, changeable and finite.***
- ***Intangible things are eternal, unchangeable and infinite.***

If tangible things are made from intangible things,

And...

Intangible things are eternal, but tangible things are temporal...

...then it stands to reason that *intangible things are more powerful than tangible things*.

This is the complete opposite from what we have been *conditioned* to believe.

THE KINGDOM WITHIN

I call heaven the **'inner world'** because, contrary to common thinking, heaven is a dimension experienced from *within*. One of the most profound statements Jesus made was that *the Kingdom of God is within you!*

Now when He was asked by the Pharisees when the kingdom of God would come, He answered them and said, "The kingdom of God does not come with observation; nor will they say, 'See here!' or 'See there!' For indeed, the kingdom of God is within you."
- Luke 17:20-21

God's Kingdom *is not in the sky* or anywhere in your outer world. The Kingdom of God, His mind, presence and reality is *within you!*

> **We are more spiritual than physical.**
> **More infinite than finite.**
> **More divine than human.**

Heaven is your inner world! Unfortunately, many of us live a life so immersed in the theater of physical reality that we are unaware of the immense power, wisdom, and infinite possibilities that lie within. The

'God realm' is *within you*. That is why the Bible is full of examples where God speaks to men and women from the inner sanctum of *dreams and visions*. Paul wrote of a dramatic experience where he was *'caught up'* to the **'third heaven.'** An experience so real, he could not tell if he was in his body or not!

It is doubtless not profitable for me to boast. I will come to visions and revelations of the Lord: I know a man in Christ who fourteen years ago - whether in the body I do not know, or whether out of the body I do not know, God knows - **such a one was caught up to the third heaven.** *And I know such a man - whether in the body or out of the body I do not know, God knows - how* **he was caught up into Paradise** *and heard inexpressible words, which it is not lawful for a man to utter.*

- 2 Corinthians 12:1-7

Although Paul could not tell if he was in his body or not, everything he experienced was in the context of *'visions and revelations.'* Over 50 dreams are discussed in Scripture, and when people awoke, they acted on these dreams.

For God may speak in one way, or in another, yet man does not perceive it. In a dream, in a vision of the night, when deep sleep falls upon men, while slumbering on their beds, then He opens the ears of men, and seals their instruction.

- Job 33:14

God is still in the business of revealing things through dreams and visions, and although they are but a brief foray into the spiritual realm, at that moment, you can see something so profound, it can change the world.

Take, for example, the 22-year-old University of Michigan graduate who was struck in the middle of the night with a vision. He had somehow managed to download the entire expanse of the World Wide Web, retaining only its interconnected links. Upon waking, he hastily grabbed a pen and wrote down what became the basis for an algorithm. This algorithm would go on to fuel the birth of a ground breaking web search engine. That young graduate was Larry Page, and the search engine he saw in his vision became Google. Today, Larry Page is one of the richest men in the world, with a net worth of $82 Billion. His visionary encounter serves as just one among numerous instances illustrating how the course of the world can be profoundly shaped by the revelations found within dreams and visions.

MIND COMES BEFORE MATTER

We were all created to be visionaries, individuals endowed with the remarkable capacity to envision and bring into reality the future we desire. As such, our fundamental purpose in life is to manifest into our outer reality what we see in our inner world.

As mentioned earlier,

> **'THINGS WHICH ARE SEEN ARE MADE FROM THINGS WHICH ARE NOT SEEN.'**

When Paul talks about *'things which are not seen'* he is referring to that which can only be seen on the screen of our **imagination**. Sight is the faculty of the mind, not the eyes. Your physical eyes serve only as a window that gives one dimension of sight. However, it is your mind that gives meaning to the streams of light and colors that pass through your eyes. Your imagination, or what is also called *'the eyes of* *your understanding,'* are your *real eyes*, enabling you to see things that your physical eyes cannot.

Strangely enough, Paul adjures us *not* to look at **things seen**, only the things that are **not seen**. God does not want your focus to be set on how things appear or what has *already* been manifested. He wants you to focus on the things to come *(John 16:13)*.

Some may misconstrue this to mean that God does not want us to have material wealth and possessions, but that is certainly not the case. Material possessions are for our use and enjoyment. It is also a means by which we can do good to others. However, **if you focus only on what you can see with your eyes, you will miss what God wants to reveal to your mind!** Hence the Proverb,

Where there is no vision, the people perish: but he that keeps the law, happy is he.

- Proverbs 29:18 KJV

"WHAT IS THE LAW THAT ONE SHOULD KEEP?"

It is the law of the mind! The law of manifesting in your outer experience that which is displayed in your mind. That is God's way for you to have the good that you desire. '**Mind comes before matter.**' Material things are the fruit of what is first seen in the mind. Anything you want to achieve in life must be manifested through your mind. The airplane had to be first seen in the mind before it could be flown in the sky. The automobile was first seen in the mind before driven on the road. Everything around us is the product of what was first seen in the mind. There is a well known saying,

> "If you can see it in your mind,
> you will hold it in your hand."

BUYING WITHOUT MONEY

The fact that material things are the product of what is first seen in the mind is the reason why God invites us to *buy without money!*
Everyone who thirsts, come to the waters; And you who have no money, come, buy and eat. Yes, come, buy wine and milk without money and without price.

— Isaiah 55:1

Buying without money does not mean you should expect what you desire to simply materializes out of thin air! It is acquiring what you want through a *mental transaction*. Jesus said,

"Whatever you ask for in prayer, **believe that you receive it, then you will have it**" *(Mark 11:24).*

"HOW CAN YOU RECEIVE SOMETHING BEFORE HAVING IT?"

The answer lies within your **imagination**. It's within your imagination that you first receive the mental equivalent of your desires. This is confirmed when you *experience* the same emotions and gratitude for this mental equivalent as you would for its physical manifestation. When you genuinely believe that you've *received* what you've asked for, you've completed the mental transaction.

As mentioned in the prologue, the sole distinction between receiving something mentally and having it physically is time. In due course, the right opportunity will present itself for you to possess what you've received mentally. This opportunity can manifest in various forms, whether it be through finances, a gift from someone, or a multitude of other possibilities. To transliterate Jesus' words,

*"Whoever has **(mental currency)** will be given more **(in their hands)**; whoever does not have **(mental currency)**, even what they have will be taken from them." (Mark 4:25)*

ABUNDANCE VS LACK AND LIMITATION

When you anchor your beliefs in the wisdom and infinite resources of the Kingdom, you unlock the power to manifest your deepest desires *(Mark 11:24)*. You will no longer see the need to compete or take what belongs to someone else. Conversely, a mind fixated on materiality thinks in terms of lack and limitation. This paradigm of lack and limitation, based on how things *appear*, represents worldly or fallen thinking. Those who subscribe to this mindset often perceive life as a zero-sum game, where one person's prosperity must come at the expense of others.

Many even entertain the notion that if someone is rich, they probably have *'ripped off'* the poor or working class! Consequently, they label the ownership of lavish luxury items as wasteful and extravagant, advocating that such items should be 'sold and given to the poor.'

However, like Jesus, a Kingdom-minded person refrains from adopting such a scarcity mentality because they know that:

- **Nothing is wasted on them**
- **They are more valuable than any expensive luxury item**

- **Out of heaven's abundance, they can do good to the poor without the need to sell what they have.**

There is only **one reason** why a rich person should sell all that they have and give to the poor, which I will discuss later.

Undoubtedly, one of the hallmarks of the Kingdom mindset is being a *cheerful giver*. Regardless of their current financial situation, a Kingdom-minded person can give cheerfully to others, knowing that there is **more where that came from.**

At times, God requires us to give sacrificially, not to deplete our resources but to expand our capacity for receiving more. If, however, you are of the mind that *'things are scarce,'* then you are less likely to make such sacrifices.

TRUTH V FACTS

The key to entering the Kingdom lies in *the way you think*. How you think will determine what you see, and what you see will determine what you experience. God's desire is for you to align your thinking with His, to adopt **the mind of Christ**, so you may see and experience life from Heaven's perspective.

Where others saw lack and scarcity, Jesus saw prosperity and abundance. Where others saw sickness and disease, Jesus saw health and well-being. Even when confronted with Lazarus' death, Jesus referred to it as sleep! When you see and do things from Heaven's perspective, your everyday life will reflect the *'truth'* despite the facts.

Spiritually speaking, truth and facts are not always the same.

- **Facts are the reality of the physical outer world.**
- **Truth is the reality of the Spirit.**
- **Facts are temporal and can be changed.**
- **Truth is eternal and unchangeable.**

Throughout His earthly ministry, Jesus demonstrated to thousands upon thousands how *'the facts'* can be changed by '**the truth,**' regardless of how grim or irrefutable those facts appeared. The facts may indeed have killed Lazarus, but it was 'the truth' that had the final say, resurrecting him back to life.

When 'truth' is put into action:

- **The blind will receive their sight**
- **The lame will walk**
- **The lepers will be cleansed**
- **The deaf will hear and**
- **The dead will be raised!**

These are just a fraction of heavenly realities that can be manifested on the earth. The truth, therefore, is **the power to change the facts.**

God said,

"Let the weak say I am strong." In other words, **"Let truth supersede the facts."** By that principle, we can also say, **"Let the sick say I am well"** or **"Let the poor say I am rich!"**

No situation or circumstance in this earthly life is *'set in stone.'* The tangible realities of this physical world are malleable to the intangible realities of Heaven. We need only align our beliefs and thinking to 'truth.'

We must, therefore, beware of the doctrine of the Pharisees and the Sadducees, avoiding a mindset that relies solely on materiality and outward appearances. That is why Paul urges us not to be conformed to the priorities of this world. That being:

- **The lust of the eyes**
- **The lust of the flesh and**
- **The pride of life...**

...all of which are based on how things appear.

To reiterate, a mind framed by outer appearances and materiality thinks in terms of lack and limitation. Surprisingly, contrary to the prevailing societal conditioning, God's reluctance toward excessive materialism is rooted in His desire to safeguard you from becoming spiritually, emotionally, and financially bankrupt! God wants you to be rich - inwardly and outwardly!

> **THE REASON GOD DOES NOT WANT YOU TO BE SO MATERIALISTIC IS TO PREVENT YOU FROM BECOMING BANKRUPT!**

Through your union and communion with Him, in the confines of your heart, He wants to reward you openly, giving you exceeding, abundantly more than you ask or think *(Ephesians 3:20)*. However, that is impossible if your mind is set on materiality and keeping all that you have!

Once you grasp that the Kingdom of God resides *within you* and recognize that **"mind comes before matter,"** heaven's treasure will be open to you. Irrespective of your financial status, God will meet your needs in accordance with His vast riches within you. Ultimately, you will prosper!

CHAPTER 11
WHERE IS YOUR TREASURE?

"Lay up for yourselves treasures in heaven, where neither moth nor rust destroys"

One can only imagine the frustration that Jesus must have felt when His disciples misinterpreted His cautionary words regarding the doctrine of the Pharisees, as a rebuke for forgetting to bring bread!

"Do you not yet understand or remember the five loaves of the five thousand and how many baskets you took up? Nor the seven loaves of the four thousand and how many large baskets you took up? **How is it you do not understand that I did not speak to you concerning bread?"**

- Mathew 16:9-11

Despite witnessing numerous miracles, the disciples still thought in terms of **lack and limitation.** What's even more disheartening is that they mistakenly believed Jesus was upset with them for *not bringing bread,* implying that He shared the same limited mindset. Unfortunately, Jesus is still misunderstood by those who fail to interpret His words within the broader context of His overall message. This is especially true when He told the Jews **"not to lay up for themselves treasures on earth."**

"Do not lay up for yourselves treasures on earth, *where moth and rust destroy and where thieves break in and steal; but lay up for yourselves* **treasures in heaven***, where neither moth nor rust destroys and where thieves do not break in and steal.* **For where your treasure is, there your heart will be also."**

- Matthew 6:19-21

If we take a *literal* view of the above text, Jesus appears to be saying we should not have any **material riches** laid up for ourselves. Indeed, that is the view many Christians subscribe to. However, when Jesus speaks of treasure, it is never with reference to money and riches, but instead **the treasure of your heart.**

For every tree is known by its own fruit. For men do not gather figs from thorns, nor do they gather grapes from a bramble bush. A good man out of the **good treasure of his heart** *brings forth good; and*

> **YOUR LIFE IS A PERFECT REFLECTION OF THE STATE OF YOUR HEART.**

*an evil man out of the **evil treasure of his heart** brings forth evil. For out of the **abundance of the heart** his mouth speaks.*

- Luke 6:44-45

Your heart, also known as the subconscious mind, serves as the center of your spiritual and physical existence. It acts as the mirror reflecting the essence of who you are, how you see yourself, and what you attract or manifest in your life. This dynamic is reflected in the well-known proverb:

'As he thinks in his heart, so is he.'
(Proverbs 23:7)

In the original Greek text, the word *'treasure'* is denoted by *'thesauros.'* This term is the root of the English word *'Thesaurus.'* Thesauros refers to a casket, receptacle, or storehouse designed to safeguard precious valuables. It's important to note that 'thesauros' itself isn't the treasure but the place where treasure is kept.

"SO, WHAT IS THE 'TREASURE' OF YOUR HEART?"

Well, as stated many times in the book of Jeremiah, and in various other books in the bible, the thing of great value lying deep within your heart, is *imagination*. More specifically, the imagination of *the thoughts* of your heart.

*O Lord God of Abraham, Isaac, and Israel, our fathers, keep this forever in the **imagination of the thoughts of the heart** of Your people, and fix their heart toward You.*

1 Chronicles 29:18

THOUGHTS ARE THE SEEDS OF LIFE

We live in a world intricately woven by the fibers of thought. Just like any other seed, thoughts require fertile soil in which to germinate, and your heart serves as that very soil. According to Luke 6:45, there is **'Good treasure'** and **'Evil treasure'** within the heart. This distinction can only be attributed to the types of thoughts one embraces.

When life appears to be working *against you*, it often results from your heart being tainted by toxic thoughts. Conversely, if you find success in every aspect of life, it's because your heart has an abundance of positive and godly thoughts. Most intriguingly, whether good or evil, toxic or divine, Jesus regards the thoughts of your heart as **'treasure.'**

Not only does your heart store your *own* thoughts, it can also house God's thoughts. As a man or woman created in the image of God, you possess the potential to *think like God*. A single thought from God—an idea, a burst of inspiration—can utterly transform your life. God's thoughts are *His* reality, and when you align your thinking with His, **His reality becomes your own.** Consequently, what may seem impossible to others becomes *'very'* possible for you.

Unfortunately, some believe that thinking like God is unattainable, even sacrilegious, and might quickly quote from the book of Isaiah:

"For My thoughts are not your thoughts, nor are your ways My ways," says the Lord. "For as the heavens are higher than the earth, so are My ways higher than your ways, and **My thoughts than your thoughts"**

- Isaiah 55:8-9

However, it's crucial to note that God didn't express this to create a distinction between Himself and us. Instead, it serves to highlight our fundamental problem—the depth to which our thoughts have fallen. Jesus, who embodies the mind of God, stated:

If you abide in Me, and My words abide in you, you will ask what you desire, and it shall be done for you (John 15:7).

To the degree that the word of God frames your thinking is the degree to which you can manifest divine life. That is, in essence, the good news of the Kingdom. The spiritual terminology for a mind that is the storehouse of divine thoughts is **'Treasure in Heaven!'** Therefore, laying up treasure in heaven requires one to store God's word or thoughts in their heart. God said to Joshua,

*This Book of the Law shall not depart from your mouth, **but you shall meditate in it day and night,** that you may observe to do according to all that is written in it. For then you will make your way prosperous, and then you will have good success.*

- Joshua 1:8

God's thoughts are the **'incorruptible seed'** that can only produce **'good success.'** It is for this reason that Jesus wants us to lay up treasure in heaven - by meditating on His word. Your treasure in heaven can be manifested into all the good that God desires for you - love, joy, success, freedom, peace, prosperity, health, and wealth. Your treasure in heaven will make you rich on the earth!

> **"IF LAYING UP TREASURE IN HEAVEN ENABLES ONE TO BECOME MATERIALLY RICH, WHY DOES JESUS WARN US NOT TO LAY UP FOR OURSELVES TREASURES ON EARTH?"**

> **GOD WANTS YOU TO HAVE TREASURE YOU CANNOT LOSE!**

Laying up treasures on earth refers to the mind that seeks *security* in the accumulation of earthly possessions. But as previously explained, this will only lead to lack and limitation. Jesus wants us to have the good that we desire. The only reason He gives to why we should not lay up treasure on earth is that it is **subject to theft or decay.** Therefore, His objection is not to us *having* material wealth; but *losing* it!

GOD WANTS YOU TO HAVE TREASURE YOU CANNOT LOSE!

The best way to achieve this is by laying up for yourself the treasure of God's thoughts in your heart. This treasure is not meant to be stored for use after death but to be utilized right here and now. God desires for you to live life abundantly in this world and in the world to come.

BEING RICH V BEING WEALTHY

Those who have 'treasure in heaven' possess something far more valuable than any precious stone; **they possess wealth.** If you aspire to lead a prosperous life, your aim should be to attain wealth, not just riches. While a millionaire may be considered rich, true wealth transcends material abundance. A rich person may have an abundance of money and possessions, but a wealthy individual possesses the means to prosper regardless of circumstances. As mentioned earlier, Joseph was a prosperous man, even as a slave. This was because of his *inner wealth*. As a result, it was only a matter of time before the wealth within him manifested, transforming him into the rich and influential man he became.

If a wealthy person were to, by chance, lose their wealth, they possess the means to rebuild it. On the other hand, if a rich person loses their riches, it's highly unlikely they will ever recover what they've lost. The distinction lies in the fact that riches can be lost, but wealth endures. Many stories abound of those who won tens or even hundreds of millions of dollars in lotteries, only to swiftly squander their winnings through extravagant spending and poor financial decisions. Not only did they lose their newfound riches, but many also found themselves deeper in debt than they were before, with their personal lives in utter disarray. They were rich **but not wealthy.**

So, the primary distinction between a rich person and a wealthy person lies in **sustainability.** Wealthy people cultivate a lifestyle that enhances the probability of their ongoing success. They seek smarter ways to work, freeing up their time for what truly matters. Wealthy individuals prioritize **long-term economic growth,** driven by purpose and passion rather than greed. While being rich and indulging in a luxurious lifestyle may appear enticing from the outside, without wealth, such a lifestyle is likely to be short-lived.

THE RICH AND THE POOR

The Bible often portrays the rich in a negative light, which has unfortunately led many to believe it is ungodly to be rich.

There is one who makes himself rich, yet has nothing; and one who makes himself poor, yet has great riches.

- Proverbs 13:7

Woe to you who are rich, for you have received your consolation.

- Luke 6:24

Then Jesus said to His disciples, **"Assuredly, I say to you that it is hard for a rich man to enter the kingdom of heaven.** *And again I say to you, it is easier for a camel to go through the eye of a needle than for a rich man to enter the kingdom of God."*

- Matthew 19:23-24

However, it is important to understand that in many instances, when the Bible speaks of *'the rich,'* it is a **metaphor** for those whose trust and security lies in the limited resources of *materiality* rather than in the unlimited resources of the Kingdom.

The rich man's wealth is his strong city, and like a high wall in his own esteem.

- Proverbs 18:11

"Here is the man who did not make God his strength, **But trusted in the abundance of his riches,** And strengthened himself in his wickedness."

- Psalm 52:7

In one of His parables, Jesus spoke of a rich man's land that produced more than what he could store at the time. He decided that he would tear down his barns and build a *bigger* one. Saying to himself:

"Soul, you have many goods laid up for many years; take your ease; eat, drink, and be merry."

However, God admonished him saying,
'Fool! This night your soul will be required of you; then whose will those things be which you have provided?'

- Luke 12:19-20).

The rich man's condemnation *did not* stem from the wealth that he possessed but because of his **state of mind,** placing his security in his 'possessions' rather than in 'the source' of his possessions.

This admonition of *'the rich'* has little to do with a person's wealth and everything to do with their mindset—specifically, a mindset of lack and limitation. This applies whether they are materially wealthy or financially poor.

Conversely, in many instances, Jesus' use of the word, *'poor,'* or *'poor in spirit,'* served as a *metaphor* for those who place their trust in God. As a result, such individuals possess **the mind of abundance** - a state of mind that you can have whether you are materially rich or financially poor.

PUT YOUR TRUST IN GOD

God wants you to prosper and have all the good that you desire. However, achieving your desires should originate from your trust in Him, putting mind before matter.

"Blessed is the man who trusts in the Lord, and whose hope is the Lord. ***For he shall be like a tree planted by the waters,*** *which spreads out its roots by the river,* ***and will not fear when heat comes;***

But its leaf will be green, and will not be anxious in the year of drought, nor will cease from yielding fruit."

- Jeremiah 17:7-8

When we manifest things from the spiritual realm into the physical world, they transition from being **eternal** to becoming *finite* and temporal. This reveals the fallacy of putting one's trust in material things.

As mentioned before, material things are meant for our use and enjoyment, not for our security. Our security lies in God, whose Kingdom resides within us. When your mind is enriched with the good treasure of God's thoughts, you can manifest the life you desire.

CHAPTER 12
THE SPIRIT OF WISDOM

"And thou shalt speak unto all that are wise hearted, whom I have filled with the spirit of wisdom"

Your mind is your most valuable asset, and when harnessed effectively, it will cause you to prosper. This is precisely why it's essential to *'lay up for yourself, treasures in heaven'* by renewing your mind to the way God thinks. The wealth derived from God's wisdom surpasses the worth of silver, gold, or any other material possession. Even if it required you to sacrifice all you possess to attain it, you would still find yourself in a superior position compared to those who are devoid of it, even the rich. This is because true wealth is wisdom.

Happy is the man who finds wisdom, and the man who gains understanding; for her proceeds are better than the profits of silver, and her gain than fine gold. **She is more precious than rubies, and all the things you may desire cannot compare with her.** *Length of days is in her right hand, In her left hand riches and honor. Her ways are ways of pleasantness, and all her paths are peace. She is a tree of life to those who take hold of her, and happy are all who retain her.*

The Lord by wisdom founded the earth; by understanding He established the heavens. By His knowledge the depths were broken up, and clouds drop down the dew.

- Proverbs 3:13-20

Wisdom is God's modus operandi. It is the means by which He brought the world into existence. By wisdom, kings reign, and princes decree justice. Even before he was endowed with divine wisdom, King Solomon was wise enough to ask God for wisdom rather than riches. As a result, God not only granted him wisdom riches but also what he did not ask for, wealth, riches, and fame exceeding that of any king before or after him *(2 Chronicles 1:9-12).*

Wisdom holds the power not only to amass wealth but also to guide your life. It will give you discernment and help you make the right decisions, especially in your dealings with others. Indeed, **you are not wealthy if you cannot forge successful relationships with others,** especially those who can open doors for you. That could well be why Jesus endorses the use of unrighteous mammon to build friendships.

Additionally, wisdom empowers you to attain your life goals more swiftly by working smart rather than working hard. Hence the proverb:

"If the ax is dull, and one does not sharpen the edge, then he must use more strength; but wisdom brings success."
- Ecclesiastes 10:10

TRUE WISDOM

Our perception of wisdom should transcend the confines of mere sound judgment or intellectual knowledge. WISDOM IS SUPERNATURAL. The ancient Hebrews understood this truth, which is why they associated the miraculous deeds of Jesus with wisdom.

And when the Sabbath had come, He began to teach in the synagogue. And many hearing Him were astonished, saying, "Where did this Man get these things? **And what wisdom is this which is given to Him, that such mighty works are performed by His hands!"**
- Mark 6:2

All the miracles of the Bible were an expression of wisdom, whether performed by Jesus, Moses, Elijah, or Elisha. Even the Magi were called *'Wise men'* because they understood the spiritual nature of wisdom.

SO, WHAT IS TRUE WISDOM?

To find the answer, let us again use the law of first mention. Wisdom first appears in the Bible when God told Moses to speak to the **wise-hearted**.

The Spirit of Wisdom

"And thou shalt speak unto all that are wise hearted, whom I have filled with the spirit of wisdom, that they may make Aaron's garments to consecrate him, that he may minister unto me in the priest's office."

- Exodus 28:3 KJV

The people described as *'wise hearted'* in scripture are the artisans. As previously explained, artisans are highly talented individuals with particular creative skills such as painting, embroidery, engraving, carpentry, and other creative work. However, their essential skill lies in their ability to manifest what they see with their imagination. Once an image is formed in their minds, they materialize it through the skillful application of knowledge and understanding. It was this ability that made the artisans so essential to Moses. Not just because of their creativity but also their ability to manifest his God-given vision. Like all visionaries, Moses was tasked with the responsibility of materializing on earth what exists in heaven. In this case, it was the tabernacle.

...there are priests who offer the gifts according to the law; who serve the copy and shadow of the heavenly things, as Moses was divinely instructed when he was about to make the tabernacle. For He [God] said, "See that you make all things according to the pattern shown you on the mountain."

- Hebrews 8:4-5

It was of vital importance that the tabernacle be reproduced exactly as revealed. That's because everything about the tabernacle bore profound symbolic significance. From the furnishings and fabrics to the colors and even the wooden pegs, each component held deep symbolic value. That is why Moses shared his vision with individuals God had given a **spirit of wisdom**. Individuals spiritually endowed to capture his vision. God, in His divine plan, left nothing to chance. He imbued Bezaleel and Aholiab with the Spirit of wisdom, empowering them to create intricate artistic designs using precious metals like gold, silver, and bronze. They were entrusted with the task of crafting jewels for settings and fashioning detailed wood carvings.

All the furnishings and regalia for the tabernacle, including:

- **The tabernacle of meeting,**
- **The ark of the Testimony,**
- **The mercy seat that is on it,**
- **The furniture of the tabernacle,**
- **The table and its utensils,**
- **The pure gold lampstand with all its utensils,**
- **The altar of incense,**
- **The altar of burnt offering with all its utensils,**
- **The laver and its base,**
- **The garments of ministry,**
- **The holy garments for Aaron the priest and the garments for his sons,**

were all meticulously designed and created by artisans anointed with the Spirit of wisdom. Even the women who spun yarns of goats hair with their hands were stirred in their hearts with wisdom *(Exodus 31 and 35)*.

RECOGNIZE WHAT YOU HAVE

> **EVERYTHING THAT YOU EXPERIENCE IN LIFE IS A RESULT OF WHAT YOU SAW OR DID NOT SEE!**

Therefore, wisdom encompasses the creative process required to manifest ideas, images, and concepts formed or captured in the mind. It is the means by which thought becomes matter, the unseen becomes seen, and the intangible becomes tangible. Sound judgment, righteousness, and the quality of being wise all stem from the spiritual principles of manifesting what is first seen in the mind.

The Spirit of Wisdom is the supernatural gift that enables a heightened ability to perceive the hidden and the intangible with exceptional clarity. Often accompanied by knowledge and understanding, the Spirit of Wisdom has the remarkable power to unveil solutions, possibilities, and opportunities that would remain concealed to the unaided eye or mind. Indeed, the entirety of our life experiences is shaped by what we either see or do not see.

Jeremiah alluded to this profound truth when he spoke of the man who *'makes flesh his strength,'* relying solely on material and external things rather than attuning his mind to what God reveals:

*"He shall be like a shrub in the desert, **and shall not see when good comes,** but shall inhabit the parched places in the wilderness, in a salt land which is not inhabited."*

- Jeremiah 17:6

If you currently feel like you're in the wilderness while others around you are flourishing, it could well be that **you did not see when *'good'* came,** or even when you had it! Jesus said at various times,

*"Whoever has, to him more will be given, and he will have abundance; but whoever does not have, **even what he has will be taken away from him.**"*

- Matthew 13:12

HOW CAN SOMETHING BE TAKEN AWAY FROM YOU THAT YOU DON'T HAVE?

This can only happen when you fail to see or *recognize* what you already have, not just in physical life but fundamentally in your mind. John said,

"This is the confidence that we have in Him, that if we ask anything according to His will, He hears us. And if we know that He hears us, whatever we ask, we know that we have the petitions that we have asked of Him."

- 1 John 5:14-15

Simply put, whatever you ask God for, *according to His will*, is yours. If you believe it is yours *(spiritually)*, then you will have it physically. That is the abundance that you will receive. If, however, you overlook, or fail to recognize what God has made yours, then it will be taken away. Therefore, much of what you may believe to be unanswered prayer is the failure to recognize what was already yours. The fact that Jesus states this principle on numerous occasions points to how vitally important it is to recognize what you have.

> "People only give up on their dreams when they feel they do not have the opportunity to fulfill them. However, it is not the absence of opportunities that is the problem, but instead, the failure to recognize opportunities and resources embedded in their lives."

THE POWER OF VISION

Hence, the Spirit of wisdom is the **power of vision**. A vital aspect of living is overlooked when one underestimates the revelations within their own mind.

VISION IS THE BLUEPRINT FOR YOUR LIFE.

It is the inner GPS that will guide you to your destiny. It controls your choices, routines, focus, career, relationships, and ultimately how you spend your precious time. When you have a clear, compelling vision, life becomes simple; because once you know what you must achieve, you automatically know what *not* to do. As a result, vision is the key to unlocking your entire life.

Many groundbreaking discoveries, such as our understanding of molecular structures, the periodic table of elements, and numerous other world-changing revelations, have sprung from dreams and visions. Throughout history, the course of human progress has been shaped by those who learned to trust the insights unveiled within their minds.

General George Patton, renowned as one of the most accomplished military leaders in history, experienced so many strategic dreams and insights that his personal secretary became accustomed to late-night calls filled with instructions stemming from his dreams. In fact, General Patton often vested more trust in his dreams than in the intelligence provided by his officers on the ground.

Harriet Tubman, a former slave who courageously led hundreds of enslaved individuals to freedom via the Underground Railroad, attested that her dreams frequently guided her to safe houses and routes. Remarkably, she never lost a single *'passenger'* during her extraordinary journeys.

CONVERTING WHAT YOU SEE TO WHAT YOU NEED

That being said, it is not enough to see solutions in dreams and visions; it's equally important to bring those visions to life! A person who has vision but fails to manifest what they see is just a dreamer - Not a visionary! As well as enhancing your ability to see visions and dreams clearly, the Spirit of Wisdom empowers you to convert what you see to what you or others need. Converting what you see in your mind to what millions of others need or want is the key to high achievement. This single action alone has the potential to propel you towards immense success.

Larry Page became a Billionaire because he had the wisdom to convert what he saw in his dream into Google - a platform that ushered in an era where knowledge is readily accessible to all.

To reiterate, people only give up on their dreams when they feel they do not have the resources or the opportunity to fulfill them. But that is only because they do not recognize the immense power of their own minds. As long as your mind remains intact, you possess the fundamental tools needed to initiate the changes necessary to transform your life and fulfill your dreams.

CHAPTER 13
MANIFESTING THE FATHER

*The Son can do nothing of Himself,
but what He sees the Father do*

The value of your imagination extends beyond what you may readily perceive. Even eminent scientific minds like Albert Einstein regarded imagination as 'the preview of life's coming attractions.' When your imagination is imbued with the Spirit of Wisdom, it becomes a conduit for achieving the miraculous. This certainly was the case with Jesus, who, according to Isaiah, had the Spirit of Wisdom, and as a result, was able to **see what the Father was doing.**

Then Jesus answered and said to them, "Most assuredly, I say to you, the Son can do nothing of Himself, but what He sees the Father do; for whatever He does, the Son also does in like manner."

- John 5:19

Jesus' capacity to *'see the Father'* did not stem from divine visitations, burning bushes, or the spectacular manifestations often found in the Hebrew Bible. Rather, the Father was whom He perceived within His own mind. Jesus was obedient to whom He saw in His mind! Every miraculous act He performed emanated from what He saw His Father doing on the screen of His imagination. As a result, His earthly existence was a manifestation of the Father's will.

What incensed the Jewish authorities was Jesus' unequivocal declaration of being **'One with the Father,'** a statement deemed punishable by death *(John 10:30-33)*. Remarkably, Jesus never wavered or succumbed to fear despite facing the imminent threat of stoning on numerous occasions due to this assertion. Here are the several key points He made:

- **When you see the Son, you see the Father.**
- **You cannot see the Father unless you see the Son.**
- **You cannot know the Father unless you know the Son.**
- **Only the Son can reveal the Father.**

Hence, the Son is the reflection of the Father, embodying His life, character, and power. This foundational truth underscores why **Jesus could not have lived a life of poverty,** for such a life *does not* reflect the Father. Even in His parables, Jesus often depicted the Father as a wealthy landowner. The only instance in which Jesus became poor was on the cross, where He willingly bore the weight of our sins for our redemption. That in itself necessitated a temporary separation from the Father, marked by the poignant cry, *'Eloi, Eloi, lama sabachthani?'*—translated as, 'My God, My God, why have You forsaken Me?'"

WHO DO YOU THINK YOU ARE?

If the Father can only be seen through the Son, **who is the express image of the Father** *(Hebrews 1:3)*, then the person Jesus recognized as the Father could only have appeared as Himself! Thus, what Jesus saw the Father doing in the imagination of His heart, was what He saw *Himself* doing. However, in seeing Himself, He understood that He was really seeing the Father. Therefore, the mighty works Jesus did, emanated from His own *self-image*. In like manner, your life is a reflection of your self-image - the person you see yourself to be in the mirror of your heart.

As in water, face reflects face, **so a man's heart reveals the man.**
- Proverbs 27:19 -

As he thinks in his heart, **so is he.**
- Proverbs 23:7 -

Keep your heart with all diligence, for out of it spring **the issues of life.** *- Proverbs 4:23 -*

The *'issues of life'* that spring from your heart are a direct reflection of how you perceive yourself. Even the events that took place in your life that seemed to be beyond your control were the product of your own self-image. If you looked at your reflection in a mirror and saw a speck

> **IF YOUR SELF-CONCEPT IS ANYTHING OTHER THAN CHRIST, THEN YOU HAVE MISSED THE MARK!**

on your face, you would not attempt to remove the speck by wiping the mirror! What's in the mirror is merely a reflection. The true reality lies in what stands before the mirror. Similarly, your outer world is a reflection of your self-image. Rather than trying to change external circumstances, you can exert an incredible amount of control over your life and the things you attract by shaping your self-image.

In the field of personal development, life coaches, motivational speakers, and the like, often encourage us to embrace a positive self-image and strive to become the best version of ourselves. While this is a step in the right direction, when God said, *"Let Us make man in our image,"* it was CHRIST whom He had in mind.

CHRIST IS THE ULTIMATE YOU!

His earthly ministry served as a profound demonstration of your true nature. That is why He said,

"Most assuredly, I say to you, he who believes in Me, the works that I do he will do also; and greater works than these he will do, because I go to My Father" (John 14:2).

While you possess the capacity to shape your own self-image, if your self-concept deviates from anything other than Christ, you have *'missed the mark,'* falling short of God's glory. As Paul elucidates, **God has reconciled humanity to Himself through Christ** *(Romans 5:10)*. It is only for humanity to realize this truth!

Jesus encapsulated this reconciliation with the Father with these words:

*"I am in my Father, you are in me, and **I am in you.**"* (John 14:20).

Oneness with Christ brings you into oneness with the Father. By identifying with Christ and embracing His Spirit, you align with your divine identity as a Son of God.

> *But he that is joined unto the Lord is **one spirit**.*
> *- 1 Corinthians 6:17*

> *For you are all **sons of God** through faith in Christ Jesus.*
> *- Galatians 3:26*

> *For as many as are led by the Spirit of God, these are **sons of God**.*
> *- Romans 8:14*

> *Behold what manner of love the Father has bestowed on us, that we should be called **sons of God**! Therefore, the world does not know us, because it did not know Him.*
> *- 1 John 3:1*

> *Beloved, now are we the **sons of God**, and it does not yet appear what we shall be: but we know that, **when he shall appear, we shall be like him**; for we shall see him as he is.*
> *- 1 John 3:2*

ONE WITH THE FATHER

'Son of God' is a gender-neutral term that transcends the conventional parent-child relationship. To be a Son of God implies not only that you recognize God as your Father but, more importantly, that God acknowledges you as His Son. While many may call God 'Father' as a term of endearment, in the ancient Jewish context, referring to God as one's Father meant making oneself *equal with God*.

But Jesus answered them, "My Father has been working until now, and I have been working." Therefore, the Jews sought all the more to kill Him, because He not only broke the Sabbath, but also said that **God was His Father, making Himself equal with God***.*

- John 5:17-18

What the Jewish tradition perceived as blasphemy was, in truth, a recognition of divine identity. To be a Son of God is to be in unity with God because the Father and Son are one. It only becomes sinful when one believes they are equal to God while perceiving themselves as *separate* from God. Viewing oneself as separate from God is the fundamental error in human thought and self-image. This is precisely why Paul encourages us to adopt the mindset of Christ:

Let this mind be in you which was also in Christ Jesus, *who, being in the form of God,* **did not consider it robbery to be equal with God**, *but made Himself of no reputation, taking the form of a bondservant, and coming in the likeness of men.*

- Philippians 2:5-7

On a subconscious level, your self-image reflects your perception of God. This interconnectedness is why your outer world is so malleable to the way you think. Unfortunately, many of us suffer from a poor self-image, and the image of God in us is either distorted, fragmented, marred, or broken! As a result, we live broken lives in a broken society.

Thankfully, God has paved the way for the shattered pieces of His image within us to be restored through Christ, who is the **complete picture** of our ultimate selves.

*For whom He foreknew, He also predestined to be conformed to the **image of His Son**, that He might be the firstborn among many brethren.*

- Romans 8:29

*He Himself gave some to be apostles, some prophets, some evangelists, and some pastors and teachers, for the equipping of the saints for the work of ministry, for the edifying of the body of Christ, till we all come to the unity of the faith and of the knowledge of the Son of God, to a perfect man, to the measure of the stature of **the fullness of Christ**.*

- Ephesians 4:11-13

WHAT DO YOU SEE YOURSELF DOING?

As a Son of God, you must also manifest the Father, for God has called us to be *unique* **expressions of Himself**. To do this, you must also *see* what the Father is doing. The question is,

"WHAT GREAT ENDEAVOR DO YOU SEE YOURSELF DOING?"

The great things you see yourself achieving in life, is in fact, what the Father is doing! Like Jesus, you must recognize that the person resembling you in a God-given vision is the Father at work.

As previously mentioned, you are called to be a unique expression of the Father. As such, you must know who God is, within you, and as you, rather than trying to emulate someone else's perception and manifestation of the Father. Your expression of the Father may be as a CEO of a global company, an award-winning actor or actress, a best-selling Author, a pioneering inventor, a billionaire philanthropist, a prime minister, a fashion designer, a publisher, a Michelin-star chef, an architect, a nurse, a craftsman, a teacher, and in all the marvelous professions that contribute to enhancing and transforming our lives.

Don't be afraid to step out to achieve your big dream, because it is what the Father is doing in and as you.

Be obedient to the passion, vision, and desire God has placed in your heart, and what you see yourself achieving in your mind.

Never let the opinions of others stifle your dream.

CHAPTER 14
THE LESSON FOR THE RICH YOUNG RULER
PART TWO

"Blessed is the man who trusts in the Lord, and whose hope is the Lord"

Considering all that has been said in the previous chapters, you may now look at the rich young ruler's encounter with Jesus from a different perspective than the purveyors of the virtues of poverty. Here's a reminder of that encounter:

Now as He was going out on the road, one came running, knelt before Him, and asked Him, **"Good Teacher, what shall I do that I may inherit eternal life?"** *So Jesus said to him, "Why do you call Me good? No one is good but One, that is, God. You know the commandments: 'Do not commit adultery,' 'Do not murder,' 'Do not steal,' 'Do not bear false witness,' 'Do not defraud,' 'Honor your father and your mother.'*

"And he answered and said to Him, "Teacher, all these things I have kept from my youth." Then Jesus, looking at him, loved him, and said to him,

"One thing you lack: Go your way, sell whatever you have and give to the poor, and you will have treasure in heaven; and come, take up the cross, and follow Me."

But he was sad at this word, and went away sorrowful, **for he had great possessions.** *Then Jesus looked around and said to His disciples, "How hard it is for those* **who have riches** *to enter the kingdom of God!"*

- Mark 10:17-22

The question is,

"CAN YOU HONESTLY STILL BELIEVE THAT WHEN JESUS INSTRUCTED THE RICH YOUNG RULER TO...

- SELL WHAT HE HAD
- GIVE IT TO THE POOR,
- HAVE TREASURE IN HEAVEN,
- TAKE UP HIS CROSS AND FOLLOW HIM,

...HE WAS INVITING HIM TO LIVE OUT THE REST OF HIS LIFE IN POVERTY?"

I assure you, **that was not the case!** As a matter of fact, the instructions given to the rich young ruler, which many interpret as evidence that believers should not be wealthy, was, in reality, an opportunity for him to attain *greater* than he ever had before.

I can state this with confidence because it is not in God's nature to demand so much from anyone and not give them back so much more *in this lifetime*. Jesus assures us that,

> *"No one who has left house or brothers or sisters or father or mother or wife or children or lands, for My sake and the gospel's,* **who shall not receive a hundredfold now in this time** *- houses and brothers and sisters and mothers and children and lands, with persecutions - and in the age to come, eternal life."*
>
> *- Mark 10:29-30*

It is impossible to *out-give* God, Who exalts the humble and doesn't hear your prayer unless you first believe **He is a rewarder of those who seek Him.** God is a kind and generous Father, seeking any opportunity to bless His children *lavishly*. But, unfortunately, like the wicked and lazy servant in the parable of the talents, many religious folk see Him as an *austere* man, **reaping where He did not sow and gathering where He scattered no seed** *(Luke 19:21)*. As a result, they readily embrace the most stringent beliefs about His will.

Had the rich young ruler taken the opportunity to be *mentored* by the 'Author of Life,' under His tutelage he would have:

- **Learned the secrets of his true identity,**
- **Learned the divine laws of the mind and how to manifest the good that he desires.**
- **Learned how to convert what he sees [with his mind]**

to what he needs [in his hands].
- Learned how to use the power of his tongue to change the facts with the truth.
- Learned to live a life of vision.

Ultimately, he would have learned how to *manifest* the Father!

You may ask,

"WHY THEN DID JESUS TELL THE RICH YOUNG RULER TO SELL WHAT HE HAD AND GIVE TO THE POOR?"

First and foremost, when Jesus provided that specific instruction to the young man, *He did so out of love.* He was not trying to entrap him so He could prove how greedy rich people are! Neither was He trying to disprove that he was not *perfect* concerning the law. In fact, when Jesus assessed and scrutinized his character, He identified that there was only *'One thing'* missing. How, many of us can honestly say that Jesus would only find 'one thing' lacking in us? The young man was as sincere as he could be but lacked one thing, that being - total trust in God!

TRUST IN GOD

Blessed is the man who trusts in the Lord, and whose hope is the Lord. For he shall be like a tree planted by the waters, which spreads out its roots by the river, and will not fear when heat comes; **But its leaf will be green, and will not be anxious in the year of drought,** *nor will cease from yielding fruit.*

- Jeremiah 17:7-8

Trusting God is the hallmark of spirituality, the beginning of wisdom, and the key to successful living. Only through trust in God one can transcend the tumultuous aspects of physical existence. Indeed, those who place their trust in God can expect to be *fruitful* in all seasons! In the same way, Jesus was able to sleep peacefully on a boat amidst a storm, when you trust in God, you too can find serenity even in the face of daunting challenges.

As demonstrated by Elisha, trusting in God opens your eyes to the reality that there are more who are with you than against you, both spiritually and physically. This trust allows you to rely on the unlimited resources of the *Kingdom within you* to come to your aid and meet your needs.

*When the servant of the man of God arose early and went out, there was an army, surrounding the city with horses and chariots. And his servant said to him, "Alas, my master! What shall we do?" So he answered, "Do not fear, **for those who are with us are more than those who are with them.**" And Elisha prayed, and said, "Lord, I pray, **open his eyes that he may see.**" Then the Lord opened the eyes of the young man, and he saw. And behold, the mountain was full of horses and chariots of fire all around Elisha. -*

2 Kings 6:15-17

Ultimately, trust in God serves as the master key to manifestation. When you possess unwavering confidence in God, you hold the assurance that what you ask for has already been granted!

*Now, this is the confidence that we have in Him, that if we ask anything according to His will, He hears us. And if we know that He hears us, **whatever we ask, we know that we have the petitions that we have asked of Him.***

-1 John 5:14-15

You can have anything you ask for according to His will, just by knowing that *God has heard you!* That is the level of trust God wants you to have in Him. Take some time to think about this profound truth because that alone can transform your life.

ETERNAL LIFE

Trust in God is what makes your mind fertile for *treasure in heaven!* As previously explained, treasure in heaven exemplifies the mind that thinks according to the word of God. When your mind has been renewed to the way God thinks, you can have what you desire! To think like God is to be like God, and to be like God is to *live like God*, and to live like God is to live as Christ. The life of Christ is **eternal life**, the very life God has embedded in our hearts.

He has made everything beautiful in its time. **He has also set eternity in the human heart;** *yet no one can fathom what God has done from beginning to end.*
- Ecclesiastes 3:11

'And this is eternal life, that they may know You, the only true God, and Jesus Christ whom You have sent.'
- John 17:3

Christ is the embodiment and ultimate expression of eternal life. Therefore, to inherit eternal life is to inherit Him. That is why, to the dismay of His would-be followers, He said,

"Whoever eats My flesh and drinks My blood has eternal life, and I will raise him up at the last day" (John 6:54).

Although the *literal* interpretation of this statement caused many of His disciples to leave Him, it was the only way He could express the fact that '**He is Eternal life!**' Therefore, what Jesus offered the rich young ruler was precisely what he had asked for: the opportunity to inherit **eternal life** by living **the Christ life**. Not a life of lack and scarcity but one filled with joy, peace, success, health, and *abundance*.

A DIRECT PATH

Jesus wanted the young man to have what he asked for but He recognized that the young man's personal adherence to the law did nothing to renew his mind to divine thinking! **He had treasure on earth but lacked treasure in heaven!** Despite his material riches, his mind was rooted in 'lack and limitation,' cutting himself off from the *'true riches'* that emanate from total trust in God.

In response, Jesus offered the young man a clear path to having 'treasure in heaven,' so he could manifest the life he longed for. This path represented a **paradigm shift** from trust in riches to total trust in God, transitioning from self-sufficiency to **divine reliance**, and evolving from 'working with his hands' to 'working with his mind.'

All he was required to do was,

> **"Sell whatever he had and give to the poor."**

The only reason Christ would require anyone to sell all they have and give to the poor is to **reset their thinking**, enabling them to attain what they desire through total trust in God.

THE ROLE OF RICH BELIEVERS

Jesus did not tell the young man to sell what he had because he was rich! It was purely because he placed his trust in material wealth. When He said, *"How hard it is for those who have riches to enter the kingdom of God!"* he clarified that statement by saying, *"How hard it is for those **who trust in riches** to enter the kingdom of God!"*

As previously mentioned, **God wants you to have money without money having you!** This sentiment is explicitly conveyed through this command, particularly aimed at those who are rich.

*Tell people who are rich at this time not to become egotistical and not to place their hope on their finances, which are uncertain. **Instead, they need to hope in God, who richly provides everything for our enjoyment.** Tell them to do good, to be rich in the good things they do, to be generous, and to share with others.*

-1 Timothy 6:17-18 CEB

While the aforementioned command could be relevant to all who are rich, it is explicitly directed at **wealthy believers**. God expects these believers to demonstrate generosity by assisting others and financially supporting the spread of the gospel—and indeed they did. As mentioned in chapter 5, wealthy landowning believers sold portions of their land and properties to ensure that no one within the growing community of believers faced lack or need. They also opened their homes to provide sanctuary for the early church, with residences spacious enough to accommodate numerous believers for gatherings where they could break bread and receive the word of God. It was in such a house that a young man named Eutychus fell from a *third-story* window while Paul was preaching.

Such was the size of the homes in which they worshipped *(Acts 20:9)*.

Contrary to the notion that Christians should be *'poor on earth and rich in heaven,'* God addresses believers who are *presently* rich. In other words, He expects there to be believers who are rich now, *not just in heaven,* nor in the world to come.

It should also be noted that at no point does God instruct wealthy believers to sell *all* their earthly possessions to avoid the temptation of placing their trust in uncertain riches. On the contrary, if a wealthy believer continues to place their trust in God, He promises to abundantly provide everything for their enjoyment.

As explained in Chapter 11, Not all who are materially rich place their trust in riches. Conversely, not all people who are broke or materially poor place their trust in God. Therefore, selling all one's worldly possessions or refraining from owning land and properties is not a universal requirement for all believers.

Through a personal relationship with God, you must follow the Holy Spirit's leading to do what is best to cultivate total trust in God and express eternal life. In the case of the rich young ruler, the specific instruction from Jesus was to sell his possessions and give the proceeds to the poor. This action was intended to help the young man develop a deeper trust in God. Had he followed through with this directive, he could have gained far more spiritually and *materially* than he had relinquished.

The Lesson for The Rich Young Ruler - Part 2

CHAPTER 15
TAKE UP YOUR CROSS

"If anyone desires to come after Me, let him deny himself, and take up his cross daily, and follow Me"

In stark contrast to the life of poverty advocated by some religious orders, Jesus presented the rich young ruler with an opportunity to **become more** and, if he desired, to *possess more* than he had ever experienced before. You may ask,

"WHAT ABOUT THE COMMAND TO TAKE UP THE CROSS?

DOES THAT NOT REQUIRE THOSE WHO FOLLOW CHRIST TO DIE-TO-SELF, WORLDLY AMBITIONS, AND MATERIAL WEALTH?"

After all,

"WHAT SHALL IT PROFIT A MAN, IF HE SHALL GAIN THE WHOLE WORLD, AND LOSE HIS OWN SOUL?" (MARK 8:36)

Many commentators interpret the concept of *'taking up one's cross'* as a metaphor for *"death-to-self."* From this perspective, many in the church embrace a life of self-sacrifice and endure unnecessary hardships, sometimes to the extent of severing ties with friends and family. Some even reject the notions of health, wealth, and prosperity, believing that their calling is to live a life of self-denial in this world in order to attain an eternal reward in the hereafter. This viewpoint often finds support in the scripture you:

"If anyone desires to come after Me, **let him deny himself, and take up his cross daily, and follow Me.** *For whoever desires to save his life will lose it, but whoever loses his life for My sake will save it."*

- Luke 9:23-24

As previously discussed, understanding the word of God and embracing divine thinking involves seeking the inner, spiritual meaning of the scripture rather than adhering solely to its outer, literal interpretation. We must, therefore, put **mind before matter**. As the apostle Paul stated:

"The letter kills, but the Spirit gives life" - *2 Corinthians 3:6.*

When you rigidly adhere to literal interpretations you risk living a harsh and disempowered way of life. However, a believer's life need not be so harsh or emaciated, especially as the central theme of Jesus' teaching is that you can have the good you desire (love, health, wealth, peace, joy, success, and prosperity) through the Kingdom of God within!

Seek first the kingdom of God and His righteousness, and all these things shall be added to you.

- Matthew 6:33

LIFE AFTER DEATH

Indeed, the symbolism of the cross carries multiple layers of meaning in Christian theology. Although the cross was an instrument of death, it also represents the path to resurrection and newness of life. From this perspective, taking up the cross is not just about death to self but also an invitation to embrace a transformed and renewed life after surrendering one's self-will to God.

The passage from Matthew 16:24-25 emphasizes this concept:

"If anyone desires to come after Me, let him deny himself, and take up his cross, and follow Me. **For whoever desires to save his life will lose it, but whoever loses his life** *for My sake will find it."*

- Matthew 16:24-25

Paul adds to this sentiment in his profound description of the born-again experience:

I have been crucified with Christ; **it is no longer I who live, but Christ lives in me;** *and the life which I now live in the flesh I live by faith in the Son of God, who loved me and gave Himself for me.*

- Galatians 2:20

For the born-again believer, **it is Christ that lives!** As a believer you are *one* with Him, manifesting *His life* as a Son of God.

Therefore, taking up one's cross, involves putting to death several negative aspects of *self*:

- **Negative self-image,**
- **Low self-worth,**
- **False identity**
- **and the distorted perception of God**

These are elements that may have been ingrained in you from the time of your birth or early life experiences. These are the things that must die! Only then can there be a resurrection and newness of life in Christ - walking in your divine identity.

Paul puts it this way,

"Put off, concerning your former conduct, the old man which grows corrupt according to the deceitful lusts, **and be renewed in the spirit of your mind, and that you put on the new man which was created according to God,** *in true righteousness and holiness."*

- Ephesians 4:21-22

It is the 'Old Man' that must die! The old man is the mind that:

- *sees itself as separate from God.*
- *sees itself as the tail and not the head.*
- *sees itself as beneath and not above.*
- *is contaminated by the leaven of the Pharisees.*

Overall, the old man is the mind trapped in the confines of physical life, lack and limitation, and external circumstances.

In contrast, the 'New Man' represents the divine self-image, aligned with the mind of Christ and an understanding of one's true identity in Christ. Embracing this divine self-image is the key to manifesting one's desires, whether they are spiritual or material.

When Jesus said, *"What shall it profit a man if he shall gain the whole world and lose his own soul?"* He was not saying that you have to choose between the world or your soul. Instead, you must *prioritize* your soul over the world. You must **seek first the Kingdom,** putting mind before matter, embracing your divine identity. In so doing, *all things* will be added to you, *for all things are yours!*

Therefore, let no man glory in men. For all things are yours; Whether Paul, or Apollos, or Cephas, or the world, or life, or death, or things present, or things to come; **all are yours; and ye are Christ's;** *and Christ is God's.*

- 1 Corinthians 3:21-23

BOOK 3
GOOD SUCCESS

PROLOGUE
WHAT IS SUCCESS

S uccess means many things to many people. The oxford dictionary defines it as the accomplishment of an aim or purpose. Success guru, Earl Nightingale defined success as,

- The successive realization of a worthy ideal.

For many years, my personal definition of success was,

- Achieving your goals without compromising your values.

As good as these definitions may be,

> **WHERE DO YOUR GOALS COME FROM?**
> **WHOSE IDEALS ARE YOU TRYING TO ACCOMPLISH?**
> **AND MOST IMPORTANTLY,**
> **HOW DO YOU DETERMINE YOUR PURPOSE?**

If you struggle to answer these questions with confidence, then you are in danger of spending years trying to achieve goals that, when accomplished, leaves you:

Disappointed,
Dissatisfied,
Discontented,
and Unhappy!

Many have spent their entire careers adhering to someone else's definition of success, or in many cases, simply *'following the follower.'* Unwilling to be ensnared in this unending cycle, I turned to the Word of God in search of a biblical definition of success. Surprisingly, the term *'success'* appears only once in the Bible, specifically in the book of Joshua.

"This Book of the Law shall not depart from your mouth, ***but you shall meditate in it day and night,*** *that you may observe to do according*

*to all that is written in it. For then you will make your way prosperous, and then you will have **good success.**"*

- Joshua 1:8

Not only does the Bible say you can have success, but **good success** —success that emanates with the word of God. The Hebrew word for success is *'Sakal,'* and although 'success' appears just once in the Bible, 'Sakal' is employed in various contexts throughout the scriptures under different translations. Thus, I embarked on a study of all the instances where 'Sakal' is used in the Bible, leading me to a more comprehensive definition of success. This definition is likely one you have not encountered before and revolves around the three key words associated with 'Sakal':

- **Guided.**
- **Knowledge.**
- **Identity.**

Good success emerges as the outcome of being

'Guided by the Knowledge of Who You Are.'

Not the misguided identities we tend to label ourselves with, but your **divine identity** - the very image of God. A closer look at the lives of some of God's leading servants reveals that their success can be attributed to being guided by their understanding of who they were. They all received a revelation of their true identity, which fundamentally shaped the course of their lives and others.

Gideon, who first saw himself as the least in his father's house, received the revelation of being a **'Mighty Man of Valor.'** Abraham held onto the promise of being the **'Father of many nations,'** even when he was advanced in age. Once these men embraced their God-given identity, they were guided along their path of victory, prosperity, and success.

So, success is really about **manifesting your identity,** and you only have good success when you express your true identity, which is your divine identity, or what I call - THE ULTIMATE YOU.

WHY DO I SAY THE ULTIMATE YOU?

Because anyone who embraces their God-given identity can expect two things:

1. **To live beyond ordinary human limitations**
2. **To achieve what others, deem impossible**

God desires for you to embrace and express your **Ultimate Self.** To live an extraordinary life of success, power and abundance. This is the **Christ life!** The life you are promised, when you allow Christ to be Himself *in you.*

CHAPTER 16
MILK AND HONEY

"The Spirit of the Lord is upon Me, because He has anointed Me to preach the gospel to the poor"

Whether you agree or not, prosperity is the greatest incentive for much of what we do. Whether in business, personal pursuits, or even charitable endeavors, success and prosperity remain the underlying motivators. Regrettably, terms such as "success" and "prosperity" can elicit mixed reactions, particularly within religious circles. Even worse is the phrase **"prosperity gospel,"** which often conjures images of shepherds fleecing their flock! However, beyond its financial connotations, prosperity encompasses advancement, progress, and the achievement of one's goals and purpose.

When prosperity is referenced in the Bible, it is frequently accompanied by the word *'peace.'* The Hebrew term for peace is *'Shalom,'* which signifies wholeness and completeness, where nothing is missing and nothing is broken. Shalom also encompasses elements like health, security, success, happiness, wellness, and, of course, prosperity. Most importantly, shalom serves as the quintessential hallmark of God's presence—the peace that surpasses all understanding.

Therefore, true prosperity is the expression of God's presence. The Bible provides numerous examples of individuals who prospered because God was *with* them. Joseph serves as the prime example highlighted in this book:

The Lord was with Joseph, and **he was a successful man;** *and he was in the house of his master the Egyptian. And his master saw that* **the Lord was with him and that the Lord made all he did to prosper in his hand.**

- Genesis 39:2-3

Indeed, prosperity is also promised to those who meditate on and take delight in God's Word.

Blessed is the man who walks not in the counsel of the ungodly, nor stands in the path of sinners, nor sits in the seat of the scornful; but his delight is in the law of the Lord, and **in His law, he meditates day and night.** *He shall be like a tree planted by the rivers of water, that brings forth its fruit in its season, whose leaf also shall not wither;* **and whatever he does shall prosper.**

- Psalm 1:1-3

This Book of the Law shall not depart from your mouth, **but you shall meditate in it day and night,** *that you may observe to do according to all that is written in it. For then you will make your way* **prosperous***, and then you will have* **good success***.*

- Joshua 1:8

It is, therefore, crucial to cultivate a positive attitude towards prosperity and all that it entails. Not only is it central to the Abrahamic Covenant, but it also forms an integral part of the gospel.

Admittedly, many would vehemently disagree with this assertion, primarily because the gospel preached for millennia has predominantly focused on salvation from hell and the promise of eternal life. When Christians speak of being *'saved,'* that's precisely what they are referring to. However, as I will elucidate in later chapters of this book, your salvation necessitates manifesting the good you desire, right here and right now, in this present lifetime. In fact,

> **"If you are not manifesting the good you desire, you are not a disciple of Christ!"**

Unfortunately, many individuals within the church struggle to attain the good they desire, and in some instances, these desires are preached right out of them!

THE GOSPEL

In the book of Hebrews, the writer draws a profound parallel between the gospel preached by the early church and the gospel proclaimed to the children of Israel during their time as slaves in Egypt. The verse from Hebrews 4:2 underscores this connection:

*For indeed the gospel was **preached to us as well as to them** [the Hebrew slaves]; but the word which they heard did not profit them, not being mixed with faith in those who heard it.*
- Hebrews 4:2

By highlighting this parallel, the Spirit of God reveals that what the early church considered *'the gospel'* was, fundamentally, the same gospel that had been preached to the children of Israel during their captivity in Egypt. Consequently, the gospel is not exclusively a New Testament concept but rather an enduring promise from the Old Testament. Furthermore, it was a gospel proclaimed to those who were impoverished and enslaved—a message that brought hope to a generation living within a system of economic bondage. This is why Jesus and His disciples preached the gospel to *the poor*.

The Spirit of the Lord is upon Me, because He has anointed Me to preach the gospel to the poor; He has sent Me to heal the brokenhearted, to proclaim liberty to the captives and recovery of sight to the blind, to set at liberty those who are oppressed.
- Luke 4:18

Jesus answered and said to them, "Go and tell John the things you have seen and heard: that the blind see, the lame walk, the lepers are cleansed, the deaf hear, the dead are raised, the poor have the gospel preached to them. And blessed is he who is not offended because of Me."
- Luke 7:22-23

"SO, WHAT WAS THE GOSPEL THAT WAS PREACHED TO THE JEWS ENSLAVED EGYPT?"

It was the gospel of *milk and honey!!*

And the Lord said:
"I have surely seen the oppression of My people who are in Egypt, and have heard their cry because of their taskmasters, for I know their sorrows. So I have come down to deliver them out of the hand of the Egyptians, **and to bring them up from that land to a good and large land, to a land flowing with milk and honey**...
- *Exodus 3:7-8*

The promise of inheriting a land flowing with milk and honey, known as 'The Promised Land,' was the hope of the children of Israel. It was this promise that sustained them during their forty-year journey in the wilderness following their remarkable exodus from Egypt. The phrase *'flowing with milk and honey'* specifically denotes a land of abundant supply and unbridled opulence.

When the children of Israel finally reached the Promised Land, Moses sent out spies to scout the land. To confirm that the land was truly flowing with milk and honey, they returned with a cluster of grapes so enormous that it had to be carried on a pole between two men. They also brought back pomegranates and figs. Not only was the land agriculturally rich, but it also abounded in minerals and precious metals.

For the Lord your **God is bringing you into a good land,** *a land of brooks of water, of fountains and springs, that flow out of valleys and hills; a land of wheat and barley, of vines and fig trees and pomegranates, a land of olive oil and honey; a land in which you will eat bread without scarcity,* **in which you will lack nothing;** *a land whose stones are iron and out of whose hills you can dig copper.*
- *Deuteronomy 8:7-9*

Deuteronomy 8 further explains that in this land of opulence, they would:

- **Eat until they are full.**
- **Build beautiful houses and dwell in them.**
- **Increase their flocks and herds.**
- **Increase their gold and silver.**
- **Increase all that they have.**

Therefore, the gospel proclaimed to those held captive in Egypt was, indeed, **the gospel of prosperity**, as preached by Christ as **the gospel of the Kingdom**. It was the good news of liberation from a system of lack and limitation, ushering them into a realm of prosperity and abundance in Christ.

CHAPTER 17
DIVINE REST

"For if Joshua had given them rest, then He would not afterward have spoken of another day. There remains therefore a rest for the people of God"

THE MENTAL TERRITORY OF PEACE AND PROSPERITY

Although the children of Israel did indeed enter the Promised Land and experienced prosperity as God had promised, their persistent disobedience and hardened hearts prevented them from fully realizing what God had in store for them. The physical land they inhabited was but a material reflection of a much greater territory: the **mental realm** of peace, victory, and prosperity. Within this realm, they could achieve *"good success,"* the outcome of prioritizing their mind over material circumstances. This realm also offered them deliverance from toil and labor, embracing an attitude to life exemplified by what the Bible refers to as **God's rest.**

Today, if you will hear His voice: **"Do not harden your hearts***, as in the rebellion, as in the day of trial in the wilderness, when your fathers tested Me; They tried Me, though they saw My work. For forty years I was grieved with that generation, And said, 'It is a people who go astray in their hearts, And* **they do not know My ways.***' So I swore in My wrath,* **'They shall not enter My rest.'** *"*

- Psalm 95:7-11

From the foundation of the world, God created everything that would come to fruition. He accomplished this in six *'spiritual'* days and then rested on the seventh day. This is the *'rest'* that God desires His children to enter—the assurance of His finished works. God's rest embodies the peace of knowing that everything concerning your life and destiny has already been meticulously planned with a victorious outcome in mind *(Jeremiah 29:11, KJV)*. Every obstacle has been overcome, every problem has been resolved, and the best possible result has already been achieved.

Christ, Himself, *rested* in the certainty of what God had predestined for His life, even during various instances when the Jews attempted to apprehend or kill Him! One such occasion occurred while He was in the synagogue, teaching profound truths that deeply unsettled those in attendance. In response to His words, the crowd became hostile and forcibly expelled Him from the city.

Fueled by murderous intent, they led Him to the edge of a cliff, to cast Him down the precipice. Astonishingly, He miraculously passed right through the crowd and went on His way *(Luke 4:24-30)*.

"HOW WAS JESUS ABLE TO WALK AWAY FROM A CROWD SO INCENSED ON KILLING HIM?"

There is no record of either men or angels coming to His aid during this perilous moment, nor did He have to engage in a physical struggle to avoid an untimely death. The key to understanding this incident can be found in other accounts where people sought to apprehend Him due to His teachings:

Then the leaders tried to arrest him; but **no one laid a hand on him, because his time had not yet come.**
- John 7:30 NLT

Because Jesus was abiding in God's rest, nothing could deter Him from what had been predestined for His life. Therefore, the angry mob could not take His life because the hour and manner of His death had *already* been predetermined.

God has indeed predestined our lives with a predetermined, victorious outcome. However, contrary to what many may believe, **predestination is a path that we must willingly choose to follow. It is not an inevitability.** Through the exercise of our own free will, God invites you to enter into the abundant life He has prepared for you by manifesting what He has already planned and completed for your life.

FINISHED WORKS

The concept of God's rest may initially appear perplexing, particularly when it seems that God is continually at work. The wonders of nature consistently reflect God's creative hand, and miracles continue to occur in our lives, much like they did during biblical times. As many can attest,

"The blind receive their sight, the lame walk, lepers are cleansed, the deaf hear, and the dead are raised up."
— Matthew 11:5

"SO HOW DO WE EXPLAIN THESE APPARENT 'ACTS OF GOD' THAT TAKES PLACE IN NATURE AND IN OUR LIVES?"

The answer lies in the **laws and systems** that God has established. God has put in place laws and systems that bring about the manifestation of His completed works. For instance, there are laws that govern the physical world's systems, including those related to weather, the Earth's orbit, seasons, bodily functions, and much more. These laws are so precise and reliable that we can launch a spaceship to Mars with pinpoint accuracy. None of these things require God to engage in continuous work because the manifestation of *"finished works"* is achieved through the application of laws and systems.

Similarly, there are *spiritual* or divine laws that govern spiritual systems. These laws determine the **moments, situations, circumstances, and events** that influence our lives. Once again, God does not need to engage in ongoing work because the manifestation of *"the work"* occurs through divine laws and systems. The distinction lies in the fact that divine law operates through the mind, by faith.

DECREE A THING!

During their exodus from Egypt, the children of Israel witnessed some of the most astonishing miracles ever recorded in the Bible. They saw the Red Sea part, allowing them to cross safely, and then witnessed it closing behind them, annihilating the pursuing Egyptian army. They observed water gushing from a rock when they were thirsty and even saw the sun and moon seemingly halt in their courses. Despite these awe-inspiring displays of power, they struggled to grasp *'God's ways,'* which involves discerning the intentions of man's heart and rendering to each person according to their deeds *(Jeremiah 17:10)*.

Unfortunately, the children of Israel were unaware of the spiritual contract between the Spirit of God and the human heart—a divine agreement granting men and women the authority to **Decree a thing and expect it to be established** *(Job 22:28)*. Had they recognized that this contract embodied the very essence of their existence, they would have understood that:

Whosoever says to this mountain, 'Be removed and be cast into the sea,' and does not doubt in his heart, but believes that those things he says will be done, he will have whatever he says.
- Mark 11:23

Unfortunately, they remained oblivious to the truth about their identity, failing to realize that all these remarkable 'finished works of God' were subject to *their will*. The Red Sea parted when Moses stretched out his hand, and it was at Joshua's command that the sun and moon appeared to stand still. Even more profound was Moses' role during the battle against Amalek: as long as he stood on a hill with his hands raised in prayer, Israel prevailed. When his arms grew weary and he lowered his hands, Amalek gained the upper hand. Ultimately, Moses needed assistance to keep his hands raised, illustrating the direct connection between the human heart and the Spirit of God, and how divine power is subject to human command. This truth applies not only to mighty prophets like Elijah and Elisha but to all who believe. No one exemplified this truth more than the woman with the issue of blood.

Now a certain woman had a flow of blood for twelve years, and had suffered many things from many physicians. She had spent all that she had and was no better, but rather grew worse. When she heard about Jesus, she came behind Him in the crowd and touched His garment. For she said, **"If only I may touch His clothes, I shall be made well."**

Immediately the fountain of her blood was dried up, and she felt in her body that she was healed of the affliction. **And Jesus, immediately knowing in Himself that power had gone out of Him, turned around in the crowd and said, "Who touched My clothes?"** *But His disciples said to Him, "You see the multitude thronging You, and You say, "Who touched Me?"" And He looked around to see her who had done this thing.*

But the woman, fearing and trembling, knowing what had happened to her, came and fell down before Him and told Him the whole truth. And He said to her, **"Daughter, your faith has made you well. Go in peace, and be healed of your affliction."**

- Mark 5:25-34

Never before in the annals of Scripture had someone taken it upon themselves to dictate the exact manner in which they would be healed without the involvement or approval of a Prophet or Priest. However, this courageous woman, despite being considered an untouchable due to her condition, rose above the stigma of her disease and pushed her way through a crowd—a daring act that carried the death penalty by stoning for someone in her state. Consider the unwavering focus and determination required as she moved past those who were aware of her condition, those who held her in contempt, and those who believed she had no right to be there. Her intent was not to *beg* Jesus for what she needed but to *receive* what she boldly declared she would obtain.

The experience of this remarkable woman underscores the promise of 'rest' available to those willing to place their faith in God, allowing His finished works to be manifested in their lives.

Divine Rest

CHAPTER 18
MANIFESTING FINISHED WORKS

"The Son can do nothing of Himself, but what He sees the Father do; for whatever He does, the Son also does in like manner"

God's rest is not merely a choice but a divine command. Instead of living a life characterized by toil and labor, God desires for you to find solace in the certainty of His finished works. He longs for you to embrace the mindset that **you have already achieved victory.** God's intention is for you to be liberated from the anxiety and uncertainty that accompany self-reliance, allowing you to lead a life filled with purpose and *divine ease*. Thus, Jesus extends the invitation:

"Come to Me, all you who labor and are heavy laden, **and I will give you rest.** *Take My yoke upon you and learn from Me, for I am gentle and lowly in heart, and you will find rest for your souls.* **For My yoke is easy and My burden is light.***"*
- Matthew 11:28-30

Jesus led a life free from anxiety because He understood God's purpose for His life. He knew His assignment and possessed a **clear vision**. He did nothing but manifest the finished works of His Father:

"The Son can do nothing of Himself, **but what He sees the Father do***; for whatever He does, the Son also does in like manner."*
- John 5:19

As explained in chapter 13, Jesus' ability to see the Father's works was not by divine visitation or burning bushes. It stemmed from what **He saw in His mind.** Let me emphasize this once more:

"Jesus was obedient to what He saw in His mind!"

All the miraculous deeds Jesus performed originated from what He envisioned His Father doing. His entire physical existence was dedicated to manifesting the finished works of the Father. When He encountered a man who had been blind from birth, possibly even born without eyes, His disciples asked whether the man's affliction was due to his own sins or those of his parents.

In response, Jesus said:

"Neither hath this man sinned, nor his parents: but that the works of God should be made manifest in him"

- John 9:3.

> **"JESUS WAS OBEDIENT TO WHAT HE SAW IN HIS MIND."**

Many have mistakenly believed that God *made* the man blind to demonstrate His power at a predetermined time. However, this belief is far from the truth. God is not the source of sickness and disease, nor does He inflict anyone with such ailments merely to showcase His power. Jesus seized the opportunity to manifest, within the man, the finished works of God. His reference to the *"works of God"* being manifested could have applied to anyone He encountered who was suffering from an affliction.

It's vital not to limit the concept of God's finished works to physical healing and deliverance alone. As Peter reveals, God's power has provided us with everything we need for life and godliness (2 Peter 1:3). The life Peter refers to is often described as *Zoe life*—the God-kind of life, representing absolute fullness and completeness. This life embodies wholeness, with nothing missing or broken. It allows us to partake in the richness of the divine nature, encompassing attributes such as love, joy, success, freedom, peace, prosperity, health, and wealth.

Jesus invites you to learn from Him so that you can manifest the works of God in your life. Just as the Son acted in accordance with what He saw the Father doing, you are called to follow suit by:

- **Discovering what God has already done for you.**

- **Believing that it has already been done**
- **Manifesting what you see into physical reality.**

Only then can you enter into the divine life of victory, joy, and abundance.

CHAPTER 19
THE GOOD THAT YOU DESIRE

*"For God is working in you, giving you the desire
and the power to do what pleases Him"*

In this book, there has been a recurring emphasis on attaining the good that one desires. To the religious mind, this may appear to be selfish, self-centered, or even sacrilegious. However, when you truly comprehend the nature of your salvation, you'll realize that achieving the good you desire is less about your *personal wants* and more about aligning with God's desires.

> **YOUR SALVATION COMES ABOUT FROM WORKING OUT WHAT GOD IS WORKING IN YOU.**

While salvation is often linked with redemption and one's eternal destiny, it primarily encompasses victory over adversaries *(both physical and spiritual)* health, preservation, and protection. Ultimately, salvation involves deliverance from *all threats,* whether they stem from external forces or our own misguided thoughts. Indeed, we often pose as our greatest obstacle, making choices that lead to missed opportunities and unfulfilled desires.

That being said, God doesn't wish for your life to be derailed by erroneous thinking and self-centered desires. Rather, He desires that you live a purpose-driven life where your desires align with His will—a life marked by vision and destiny.

Hence, instead of offering a one-size-fits-all solution, your salvation is a tailor-made remedy crafted to overcome anything that obstructs your ability to fulfill your God-given vision. Whether it entails sickness, lack, or even the influence of others, God has provided a pathway to deliverance, and it's all in you.

Work out your own salvation with fear and trembling; **for it is God who works in you both to will and to do for His good pleasure.**

- Philippians 2:12-13

Your salvation comes about from working out what *God is working in you.* It is the dynamic of manifesting what is most desirable and pleasing to God. Everything you need for deliverance and victory, whether in your finances, health, or relationships, hinges on your ability to manifest your God-given desires.

Therefore, when I speak of you having the good you desire, I am talking about **manifesting your own salvation!**

As your desired good pertains to your salvation, it should not be taken lightly. The instruction to do so with *"fear and trembling"* underscores the seriousness of the matter. As mentioned earlier, **Christ is the true vine, and you are the branches.** The life of the vine flows into the branches. As a branch, your role is to express the vine's life by bearing fruit. The life of the vine consists of God's thoughts, and the fruit represents the manifestation of these thoughts, experienced in your heart as the good you desire.

Jesus said,

"Every branch in Me that does not bear fruit He [The Father] takes away!"

- John 15:2

He then said,

"If you abide in Me, and My words abide in you, ***you will ask what you desire, and it shall be done for you.*** *By this My Father is glorified, that you bear much fruit;* ***so you will be My disciples.****"*

- John 15:1-8

Therefore, it's erroneous to perceive pursuing the desires of your heart as selfish. Through your union with Christ, **your desires represent the seed of His Word in your heart,** sowed to be manifested for your benefit and the benefit of others. It is only when you bear fruit in this manner that you **bring glory to God** and fulfill His good pleasure. You can only be deemed a disciple of Christ when you manifest the good you desire.

You are the vessel through which the things of God are manifested, utilized, and enjoyed on Earth. Jesus proclaimed, *"All things the Father has, belong to Me,"* and through your union with Christ, they also belong to you.

CHAPTER 20
HOW GOOD DO YOU WANT GOD TO BE

◆

"Love your neighbor as yourself"

GOD IS GOOD! If you are familiar with Charismatic or Pentecostal circles, you've likely heard this statement repeated many times, instantly followed by the rapturous response, "ALL THE TIME!" Indeed, God is good *all the time*, - goodness expressed by success, joy, freedom, peace, prosperity, health, and wealth. However, this prompts some important questions:

> **"HOW 'GOOD' DO YOU WANT GOD TO BE - TO YOU?"**
>
> **"DO YOU EVEN BELIEVE HE CAN BE GOOD TO YOU AS MUCH AS HE APPEARS TO BE TO OTHERS?"**
>
> **"OR DO YOU THINK GOD HAS FAVORITES, HIS SPECIAL 'ANOINTED ONES' WHO SEEM TO GET ALL THE BLESSINGS?"**

While it might seem that God's love shines more brightly on certain individuals than on others, the truth is that *you* determine the extent of God's goodness in your life. God does not show partiality, and His goodness is available to all. The key to experiencing God's goodness lies in two of the Bible's greatest commandments.

LOVE THE LORD YOUR GOD

A lawyer, asked Jesus a question, testing Him, and saying, "Teacher, which is the great commandment in the law?" Jesus said to him,

*" **'You shall love the Lord your God with all your heart, with all your soul, and with all your mind.'** This is the first and great commandment. And the second is like it: **'You shall love your neighbor as yourself.'***

On these two commandments hang all the Law and the Prophets."

- Matthew 22:35-40

In our quest to *unlock* more of God's goodness, let's begin with a fundamental question:

"IF WE ARE TO LOVE THE LORD WITH ALL OUR HEART, SOUL, AND MIND AND THEN LOVE OUR NEIGHBOR AS WE LOVE OURSELVES, AT WHAT POINT DO WE LOVE OURSELVES?"

Between these two great commandments, it might seem that there is no specific directive to love oneself. This apparent omission could make it challenging to love our neighbor as *ourselves*. However, since God is not a God of confusion or contradiction, there must be a resolution to this apparent dilemma.

The answer is that:

'To love God is to love oneself!'

You can only fulfill the commandment to love the Lord your God with all your heart, soul, and mind by first *loving yourself*. Once you have truly loved God in this manner, you are then equipped to love your neighbor as yourself.

If the idea of loving God through loving yourself seems self-centered or egotistical, it may be because you perceive yourself as *separate* from God. As previously explained, **mankind is the visible expression of the invisible God. We were created to be the person God sees when He looks in the mirror!**

Therefore, you cannot truly love God apart from loving the person you can see—*yourself*. This was the profound truth that John conveyed when he wrote:

If someone says, "I love God," and hates his brother, he is a liar; ***for he who does not love his brother whom he has seen, how can he love God whom he has not seen?*** *And this commandment we have from Him: that he who loves God must love his brother also.*

- 1 John 4:20-21

In essence, you cannot love God, whom you have not seen, without also loving the people you can see. While you may have emotional attachments to the invisible God, your love is only genuine when it extends to those whom God embodies, *starting with yourself.* When Jesus relayed the 'greatest command' to the lawyers, He quoted the latter part of a scripture verse they were well-acquainted with. It is crucial to grasp the earlier portion of this scripture, as it provides the context and foundation for the greatest commandment.

ONENESS

"Hear, O Israel: ***The Lord our God, the Lord is one!*** *You shall love the Lord your God with all your heart, with all your soul, and with all your strength."*

- Deuteronomy 6:4-5

'Hear, O Israel: The Lord our God, the Lord is one,' is part of the Jewish prayer known as *'The Shema.'* The Shema, is a central prayer in the Jewish faith, declaring the **oneness** of God. However, while Jews interpret this oneness as one singular entity, New Testament scriptures reveal that the oneness of God is the union of multiple persons within the Godhead, consisting of the Father, the Son, and the Holy Spirit—the Trinity.

Further evidence of the triune God or multiple persons within the Godhead can be found in the Shema when examining the Hebrew words for "God is one Lord."

'Elohiym echad Jehovah'

The Hebrew word *Elohiym*, which is translated into English as "God," is *plural* in form. This plurality reflects the multifaceted nature or *expressions* of God. Elohiym is used to describe divine beings, rulers, judges, and gods. Notably, it is the same word used in Psalm 82:6 when God referred to human beings as "gods":

"I said, You are gods [Elohiym] and children of the most high."

To clarify, Elohiym does not suggest the existence of multiple Gods; rather, it signifies **the same God** expressed in various ways or entities. God's children are referred to as *"gods"* not because they are gods in and of themselves, but because of their *union* with Him. The Bible also emphasizes that anyone who is joined to the Lord becomes **one Spirit** with Him *(1 Corinthians 6:17)*. In this sense, our oneness with God can be likened to the administration of the gifts of the Spirit, as described by the Apostle Paul:

There are diversities of gifts, ***but the same Spirit.***
There are differences of ministries, ***but the same Lord.***
And there are diversities of activities, ***but it is the same God***
who works all in all.

-1 Corinthians 12:4-6

In Christ, we are all *'gifts of the Spirit.'* Our unique gifts, talents, skills, passions, and brilliance are all manifestations of the same Spirit who works in and through all, according to His divine purposes. This is why the Apostle Paul encourages us to maintain **the unity of the Spirit in the bond of peace.** In this unity, there is:

- **ONE BODY**
- **ONE SPIRIT,**
- **ONE HOPE,**
- **ONE LORD,**
- **ONE FAITH,**
- **ONE BAPTISM,**
- **ONE GOD AND FATHER OF ALL...**

...**who is above all, and through all, and in you all** *(Ephesians 4:4-6).*

God is a God of oneness, with Himself and His children. Therefore, it is in the context of oneness with God, you are to love Him, and that first requires you to love yourself! To transliterate John's point,

'YOU CANNOT LOVE GOD WHOM YOU HAVE NOT SEEN BUT HATE THE PERSON YOU SEE IN THE MIRROR'

GOD-IN-YOU

Over the past millennia, Christianity has often emphasized the idea of sin-based unworthiness, despite the fact that Christ's sacrifice on the cross has dealt with our sins, and God has chosen to remember our sins no more *(Hebrews 8:12).* Additionally, Christianity has promoted the virtue of putting others before oneself, which is commendable in many situations but can also leave one vulnerable to *abuse*.

God's greatest commandment calls for you to love the Lord *your God* by

> **LOW SELF-WORTH AND SELF-HARM IS A VIOLATION OF GOD'S GREATEST COMMANDMENT.**

loving yourself. I emphasize 'Your God' because I am referring to **GOD-IN-YOU**. God-in-You is no less a God than He is anywhere else. However, many within the church tend to give more honor and reverence to a distant God in the sky or have more faith in what God can do through pastors, prophets, and evangelists than in what the same Lord is willing to do through and within them.

Somehow the church has woefully overlooked God's ultimate plan. A plan so fundamentally important that it was shrouded in secrecy from the beginning of time, only to be revealed and made manifest to the saints. This mysterious plan, which encompasses the fullness of God's glory, is this:

CHRIST-IN-YOU, THE HOPE OF GLORY
(Colossians 1:26-27)

Unfortunately, the magnitude of Christ within you has been *subdued* by the constant bombardment of sin-based unworthiness spewing from many church pulpits. This sense of unworthiness, characterized by low self-worth and a poor self-image, leads to valuing others above oneself. Meanwhile, sin-consciousness, marked by guilt and a focus on iniquity, creates a sense of separation from the indwelling presence of God (God-in-You).

We will do well to understand Isaiah's cry:

*Behold, the Lord's hand is not shortened, that it cannot save; neither his ear heavy, that it cannot hear: But your iniquities have separated between you and your God, and your sins have hid **his face** from you,* *that he will not hear.*

- Isaiah 59:1-2

It is important to note that sin-consciousness does not hide *your* face from God. Instead, it hides *His face* from you.

A person's face is their identity, and, in Christ, **God's face is your face!** Hidden within your subconscious mind is the profound truth that God is integral to your own self-image. As a result, what you affirm about yourself echoes a profoundly on what you say about God. To deem yourself unworthy is to cast a shadow on the divine. Therefore, like the prodigal son, you must *'come to yourself,'* remembering where you came from and who you are!

- **You were created in God's image.**
- **You are the visible image of the invisible God.**
- **You are God's chosen habitation.**
- **God desires to express Himself in you and as you.**

Therefore, you should hold a higher reverence for God-in-you than any perception of God outside of you. This can only be expressed through the love you give to *yourself*. Oneness with God is epitomized by **Christ being your Ultimate Self.** When you understand your union with Him, you will realize that the greatest commandment of all is to *"Love Thyself"* because:

Self-love is God-love.

The greatest commandments, upon which the law and the Prophets hang, can be expressed as follows:

1. Love God-in-you by loving yourself.
2. Love your brothers and sisters as you love God-in-you.

While there are many situations where you should prioritize others, it should not come at the expense of *violating* the greatest commandment. Allowing yourself to be abused is a violation of the greatest commandment. Wollowing in low self-worth and harming yourself are also violations of the greatest commandment.

- Value God by valuing yourself.
- Honor God by honoring yourself.
- Love God by loving yourself.

That is how you exercise your union with God.

THE ROYAL LAW

Once you learn to love God by loving yourself, your love for God is made complete by *loving your neighbor as yourself*. This is the second great commandment, which encompasses the first commandment, for the second cannot be fulfilled without the first. That is why James referred to the second law as 'The Royal Law.'

If you really fulfill the royal law according to the Scripture, **"You shall love your neighbor as yourself,"** *you do well; but if you show partiality, you commit sin, and are convicted by the law as transgressors.*

- James 2:8-9

The Royal Law, as stated in the book of James, is presented in the context of not showing undue favoritism to others, especially with regard to how the poor were treated.

My brethren, do not hold the faith of our Lord Jesus Christ, the Lord of glory, with partiality. **For if there should come into your assembly a man with gold rings, in fine apparel,** *and there should also come in a poor man in filthy clothes, and you pay attention to the one wearing the fine clothes and say to him,* **"You sit here in a good place,"** *and say to the poor man, "You stand there," or,* **"Sit here at my footstool," have you not shown partiality among yourselves**, *and become judges with evil thoughts?*

— James 1:4

Showing undue respect or treating others according to their financial status is a grave violation of the Royal Law. When you love others as yourselves, you are, in essence, loving **God-in-them**. Therefore, not only are you doing someone a disservice when you treat them poorly, but you are also disrespecting God! You will do well to heed the words of Jesus when He spoke of how He will judge the world:

"When the Son of Man comes in His glory, and all the holy angels with Him, then He will sit on the throne of His glory. All the nations will be gathered before Him, and He will separate them one from another, as a shepherd divides his sheep from the goats. And He will set the sheep on His right hand, but the goats on the left.'

Then the King will say to those on His right hand, 'Come, you blessed of My Father, inherit the kingdom prepared for you from the foundation of the world: **for I was hungry** *and you gave Me food;* **I was thirsty** *and you gave Me drink;* **I was a stranger** *and you took Me in;* **I was naked** *and you clothed Me;* **I was sick** *and you visited Me;* **I was in prison** *and you came to Me.'*

Then the righteous will answer Him, saying, 'Lord, when did we see You hungry and feed You, or thirsty and give You drink? When did we see You a stranger and take You in, or naked and clothe You? Or when did we see You sick, or in prison, and come to You?' And the King will answer and say to them, 'Assuredly, I say to you, inasmuch as you did it to one of the least of these My brethren, **you did it to Me.**'"

- Matthew 25:31-40

Notice that *all nations* are gathered before Christ. Despite all the laws and doctrines in which humanity seeks salvation, the only law that determines whether one inherits the Kingdom or not is The Royal Law. Loving your fellow brothers and sisters is synonymous with loving God within them. Conversely, mistreating your brothers and sisters equates to mistreating God. This is precisely why the measure of a great leader is unveiled in how they treat those who have nothing to offer them.

BE GOOD TO GOD

Returning to the question of how good you want God to be, the answer lies in **how good you want to be to God!** If loving God is equivalent to loving yourself, then being good to yourself is being good to God. Jesus emphasized that the Father is glorified when we *bear fruit*. In other words, we honor God when we manifest the fruit of His thoughts - love, joy, success, freedom, peace, prosperity, health, and wealth.

The Bible reminds us numerous times that 'The earth is the Lord's and everything in it.' The gold, the silver, even the cattle on a thousand hills—all belong to Him *(Haggai 2:8, Psalm 50:10)*. However, we must remember that God is Spirit. What use could God have for material wealth if not through the enjoyment of those He inhabits? In this sense, God delights in *your joy* when you experience His goodness in your life. Therefore, when you deprive yourself of *His goodness*, you also deprive God of *your* experience of His goodness. When you shun prosperity, you deny God the joy of *experiencing* what belongs to Him.

It's crucial to realize that you and God are on life's journey together, and you take away from Him what you believe you and others should not have.

Place no limits on God's goodness in your life, for it is His good pleasure to give you **exceedingly abundantly above what you ask or think.** As the Bible says, - The *joy* of the Lord is your strength!

Don't let anything or *anyone* hinder you from embracing the goodness that God intends for you to have. The more of His goodness you manifest in your life, the more glory and joy you bring to Him.

By loving yourself, you are, in fact, loving God. Do not deprive Him of the good that He wants you to enjoy. If it appears that God's love shines more brightly in the lives of others than in yours, it is simply because He is enjoying life more fully in them than in you!

CHAPTER 21
YOUR DIVINE IDENTITY DEMANDS FOR YOU TO BE RICH

◆

"Clothe him in the best robe, put a ring on his hand and shoes on his feet"

Recently, I had the pleasure of re-watching 'Coming to America,' the iconic '80s movie starring Eddie Murphy and Arsenio Hall. Murphy portrays Prince Akeem Joffer, the crown prince of the fictional African nation of Zamunda, who travels to the USA in search of his Queen. In order to attract a woman who will love him for himself and not his immense wealth, Prince Akeem and his personal aide, Semmi, rent a squalid tenement in Queens, New York, under the guise of poor foreign students. However, Semmi grows tired of this impoverished lifestyle. Against the Prince's approval, he secretly sends a telegram to Akeem's father, King Jaffe Joffer, requesting a 'cool $1Million' because they were in *dire straits!* Unaware of his son's plan to live in such poor conditions, the King grows concerned and decides to travel to America in person to bring his son home.

Upon arriving at Akeem's apartment, he discovers, to his horror, that his son was **'At work!!'** In his anger, he accosts Semmi and reprimands him for not taking better care of his son. As punishment, the King orders Semmi to confine himself to his *'royal suite'* at the Waldorf Astoria. Although Semmi was suitably dressed, by anyone's standards, the King orders his aides to give Semmi a thorough bath and clothe him in *decent attire!* Unable to contain his joy, Semmi cries,

"Oh, thank you, your Royal Majesty!"

King Jaffe's reaction towards seeing his beloved son living below his privilege somewhat reminds me of the loving father in Jesus' parable of the prodigal son. He, too, was a man of great wealth, and upon seeing his son in the distance, returning home barefoot, dirty and in rags, rushed out and kissed him. Having wasted his inheritance on wild and excessive living, his son had fallen on hard times. Reduced to feeding pigs and perishing with hunger, *he came to himself* and decided to return home to his father.

Believing he was no longer worthy of being called his son, he hinged his hopes on his father being *merciful* enough to hire him as one of his servants. However, his cry of *unworthiness* fell on 'deaf ears,' and his father ordered his servants to **clothe him in the *best* robe,** put a ring on his hand and shoes on his feet *(Luke 15:11-22).* This act symbolized more than a change of attire; it followed the ancient custom of clothing someone in **wealth and power,** akin to what Pharaoh did when he appointed Joseph as ruler over all Egypt.

And Pharaoh said to Joseph, "See, I have set you over all the land of Egypt." ***Then Pharaoh took his signet ring off his hand and put it on Joseph's hand; and he clothed him in garments of fine linen and put a gold chain around his neck.***
- Genesis 41:41-42

By clothing his son with wealth and power, the father in the parable restored not only his son's dignity but also his **identity**.

Like the prodigal son, your divine identity demands for you to be rich! God has ignored your cries of unworthiness and has decreed that you be *adorned* with wealth and power. Just as the noble King of Zamunda did not want his son living beneath his privilege, the Most-High God does not want you to live below *your* privilege. '**You are royalty!**' Your life should be such that even a small gesture from you brings great joy, much like Semmi's elation upon learning of his impending punishment!

Like the prodigal son, you don't have to do anything to get back into your Father's 'good graces', for Christ has already accomplished that on your behalf. God's only desire is for you to *'Come to Yourself.'* To be awakened by the revelation of **His Son in you** *(Galatians 1:15-16).* To recognize and comprehend that you are more than what your circumstances may suggest.

You are greater than your color, greater than your race, and greater than society's perceptions of you. It's only when you grasp the fact that **'You Are More,'** that God can *renew* your dignity, *restore* your inheritance, and *reaffirm* your divine identity. After all, the restoration of these things is what *salvation* is all about.

CHAPTER 22
HONOR THE LORD WITH WEALTH

"Honor the Lord with all your substance and with the first fruits of all thine increase"

Given what has been discussed regarding your union with Christ and the idea that God is glorified when you manifest His goodness, I can now shed light on the critical divine law for your success, widely taught from the wrong perspective.

Honor the LORD with thy substance, and with the first fruits of all thine increase: **So shall thy barns be filled with plenty, and thy presses shall burst out with new wine.**
- Proverbs 3:9-10 KJV

Many prosperity preachers have propagated the belief that generous giving to the church or a particular ministry equates to giving to God, and by doing so, God will make you rich. This notion is often framed as, *"The more you give, the more you will receive!"* Additional scriptures cited to support this teaching include:

He who sows sparingly will also reap sparingly, and he who sows bountifully will also reap bountifully.
- 2 Corinthians 9:6

So let each one give as he purposes in his heart, not grudgingly or of necessity, for God loves a cheerful giver.
- 2 Corinthians 9:7

Regrettably, this interpretation has led to the financial detriment and ruin of many who, in good faith, gave nearly all they had. Despite their diligence in paying tithes and offerings, numerous faithful churchgoers still grapple with financial difficulties. It's essential to revisit and reassess our understanding of these principles to ensure that they align with the true essence of God's word.

"SO WHY ARE SO MANY CHRISTIANS BROKE?"

"IS THE PROBLEM DOWN TO HOW MUCH OR LITTLE THEY GIVE?"

"IS IT BECAUSE THEY GIVE WITH THE WRONG OR SELFISH MOTIVES?"

Although the above could be considered contributing factors, the truth is,

'Putting money in an offering box will not solve your financial problems!'

Don't get me wrong—I'm not suggesting that you should refrain from giving to your church or any other charitable organization. Quite the opposite, it's imperative to provide financial support to help those in need. However, the promise of financial abundance through honoring God with your substance and firstfruits is more about what you *receive* than what you give!

YOU MUST MANIFEST GOD'S WEALTH

To begin with, it's important to note that the term 'substance' in Proverbs 3:9 is translated from the Hebrew word for *wealth*. Therefore, Proverbs 3:9 is essentially calling for you to **'Honor God with your wealth!'** The proverb therefore assumes *you already possess wealth*. Consequently, the act of honoring God is not a means to *acquire* wealth but rather an expression of gratitude for the wealth you already have.

Undoubtedly, God is the Ultimate Philanthropist, and His children are called to be the same. Philanthropy is the divine calling of every believer and the ultimate purpose for becoming rich. Therefore, seek to manifest God's wealth in your life first. God has already blessed you with every spiritual blessing *(Ephesians 1:3)*. However, spiritual blessings are useless unless they are manifested into **tangible things and material wealth**. Thus, honoring God requires you to receive in your hands what He has placed in your mind.

THE FIRSTFRUITS PRINCIPLE

Secondly, the principle of honoring the Lord with the firstfruits of our increase originates from an agricultural society. In such a society, harvest time marked the culmination of hard work and time invested by farmers, and it was a time of great significance. God instructed His people to bring into *His* house, the firstfruits of their labor or business, along with what was sown in the field. This act was accompanied by the promise that their barns would be filled with plenty, and their presses would overflow with new wine. For the Hebrews, offering the firstfruits represented an investment in their future prosperity.

In the modern-day church, firstfruits have taken on a purely financial meaning and are deemed as an offering to be made above and beyond tithing. The firstfruit itself maybe:

- The first paycheck of a new job
- The first paycheck of the year
- The first portion of each subsequent paycheck
- The first portion earned from the sale of something
- The first portion of your bonus
- The first portion of a tax refund
- The first portion of each subsequent paycheck

…and so on and so forth.

The reasons stated for giving a first fruits offering also vary:

- To ensure God will bless the giver's plans for the new year
- To show sacrificial faith that God will provide
- To give thanks for God's provision
- To 'sow a seed' so that God will make the giver rich

Although the concept of the firstfruit is very much relevant to us today, there is nowhere in the New Testament where believers are required or even encouraged to give a firstfruits offering in a church service or wherever they assemble. As a matter-of-fact, the firstfruit offering holds a distinct significance from regular offerings and tithes. This is because in the New Testament, the rendering of firstfruits takes on a *symbolic* meaning where we see Paul speaking of Christ as the **"first fruits of those who have fallen asleep"** *(1 Corinthians 15:20).*

Therefore, firstfruits can encompass various aspects of one's life, such as time, money, or anything else of *personal* value. What remains unchanged is that firstfruits represent an investment in *your* future.

PAY YOURSELF FIRST

While giving firstfruits to the Lord, or the house of the Lord, has been interpreted as giving to your local church, the truth is, '*You* **are the house of the Lord.**' That is the New Testament reality of what was symbolized in the old covenant. The fundamental difference between the old and new is that the new covenant reflects the believer's **union and oneness with Christ.** Therefore, the most direct way to offer a firstfruit to the Lord is to *pay yourself first!* In so doing, you are investing in your own personal and spiritual growth, to the glory of God.

> **THE MOST DIRECT WAY TO GIVE A FIRSTFRUIT OFFERING TO THE LORD IS TO PAY YOURSELF FIRST!**

As previously mentioned, you should hold a deeper reverence for the presence of God within you than for any *external* concept of God. This reverence is expressed through the love and care you extend to yourself. Not only is paying yourself first a fundamental principle of personal finance, it also reflects the divine order of the greatest commandment and the Royal Law. Simply put, you must,

- Take care of yourself first, so you can take care of others.
- Reward yourself first, so you can bless others.
- Invest in yourself first before investing in others.

At first glance, this concept may seem self-centered or egotistical, particularly if you perceive yourself as *separate* from God. However, when you maintain a conscious awareness of your oneness with the Father through Christ, prioritizing **self-care** before caring for others becomes a mutually beneficial way of living—a true win-win scenario.

Loving yourself first, to the highest degree, enables you to love and care for others to the same extent. Importantly, this should be done with the understanding that **loving yourself is loving God.**

The Bible does not specify what amount constitutes firstfruits because the firstfruit is a *personal offering* between you and God, agreed upon between you and God, that stays between you and God! When you give to God first, by prioritizing your financial well-being, you set the stage for blessings in all areas of your life. This overarching principle applies to every facet of your life.

FIRSTFRUITS OF YOUR TIME

Without a doubt, Paul stands out as one of the most successful figures among the New Testament apostles, doing more to spread the gospel than any other. Through Paul, the Spirit of God conveyed spiritual wisdom that Jesus refrained from sharing with His disciples, due to their limited spiritual maturity at the time:

I still have many things to say to you, **but you cannot bear them now.** *However, when He, the Spirit of truth, has come, He will guide you into all truth... John 16:12-13*

HOW WAS PAUL ABLE TO KNOW AND DO SO MUCH MORE THAN THE DISCIPLES WHO SAT AND ATE WITH JESUS?

I believe it was due to the firstfruits principle of paying or investing in yourself first. **Paul's firstfruit offering was** *his time*. After his dramatic conversion on the road to Damascus, he spent three years of *exclusive* time with the Lord in the Arabian desert. It was in this time of solitude that he received the gospel through direct revelation from Christ.

But I make known to you, brethren, that the gospel which was preached by me is not according to man. For I neither received it from man, nor was I taught it, **but it came through the revelation of Jesus Christ.**

- Galatians 1:11-12

Paul spent **quality time** with God before doing what he was called to do - preaching the gospel to the Gentiles. Out of this firstfruit offering emerged the man through whom God would use to change the world.

Time is your most valuable asset. When given to God as a firstfruit offering, it yields a greater dividend than money. Therefore, invest your time in your personal and spiritual development. In doing so, you allow **God to make all grace abound to you, ensuring that you have all sufficiency in all things at all times, enabling you to abound in every good work** *(2 Corinthians 9:8)*.

CONCLUSION

To reiterate, your firstfruit giving should be done from a position of wealth rather than to attain wealth. You obviously cannot do that if you are apprehensive about becoming rich! Therefore, you should seek to:

- **Manifest the wealth God has placed inside you**
- **Honor God by investing in yourself first**
- **Give God your best by becoming the best**

In so doing, **your future will be blessed,** you will be a greater blessing to others, and you will always have the ability and the resources to do more good in the world.

CHAPTER 23
DON'T BE ON THE WAYSIDE

"There are some who trouble you and want to pervert the gospel of Christ"

As previously explained, your salvation involves manifesting the thoughts and desires that God sows in your heart (subconscious mind). This process is how God intends to bestow upon you what rightfully belongs to Him and clothe you with the wealth and power befitting your divine identity.

To achieve this purpose, God sent His word to *prosper you*.

So shall My word be that goes forth from My mouth; It shall not return to Me void, **but it shall accomplish what I please,** *and it shall prosper in the thing for which I sent it.*

- Isaiah 55:11

Your heart is *'the thing'* God's Word will prosper in, and His Word is the good news of the Kingdom. The good news of the Kingdom is the *'Seed'* that encapsulates all that pertains to restoring your wealth, influence, power, and identity in Christ. However, that seed can only bear fruit if the soil of your heart is *good*.

As identified in the parable of the sower, there are four spiritual conditions of the subconscious mind. Only *one* of those conditions will manifest divine thought. The four spiritual conditions are:

The Wayside
- Spiritual ignorance

"When anyone hears the Word of the Kingdom, and does not understand it, then the wicked one comes and snatches away what was sown in his heart. This is he who received seed by the wayside."

- Matthew 13:19

Stony Places
- Superficial and shallow-minded

"He who received the seed on stony places, this is he who hears the Word and immediately receives it with joy; yet he has no root in himself,

but endures only for a while. For when tribulation or persecution arises because of the Word, immediately he stumbles."

- Matthew 13:20-21

Among the thorns
– Easily distracted, materialistic, puts matter before mind

"Now he who received seed among the thorns is he who hears the Word, and the cares of this world and the deceitfulness of riches choke the Word, and he becomes unfruitful."

- Matthew 13:22

Good ground
– Full of faith, spiritual wisdom and understanding

"He who received seed on the good ground is he who hears the Word and understands it, who indeed bears fruit and produces: some a hundredfold, some sixty, some thirty."

- Matthew 13:23

Out of the three conditions that do not produce fruit, *'The Wayside'* is the most insidious. While the other conditions can be addressed by deepening one's trust in God...

> **"HOW DO YOU STOP SATAN FROM SNATCHING AWAY WHAT GOD SOWS IN YOUR HEART?"**

Indeed, such a scenario can only unfold when you're *predisposed* to the wiles of the enemy. Nothing renders you more susceptible to Satan's schemes than *ignorance,* especially when you lack a deep understanding of the Kingdom's paradigm and mindset.

That said,

"IS THE WORD OF THE KINGDOM SO DIFFICULT TO UNDERSTAND?"

Apparently not, for even the *'Stony heart'* person, representing those who are *shallow* in their thinking and lacking in spiritual fortitude, initially received the Word with joy. Likewise, the *'Thorny heart'* person, characterized by *materialism* must have first accepted the Word; otherwise, how could it have been choked? This observation carries profound implications because it suggests that the 'Word of the Kingdom' or the 'Gospel of the Kingdom' can appeal not only to people of faith but also to **those leading superficial, materialistic lives.**

BUT IS THAT REALLY A SURPRISE?

After all, why wouldn't anyone rejoice upon hearing the message that they can attain love, joy, success, peace, freedom, good health, and wealth through the restoration of their divine identity?

SO, WHY WOULD THOSE ON THE WAYSIDE FAIL TO UNDERSTAND SUCH A MESSAGE?

The only plausible explanation is that "Waysiders," — individuals predisposed to the wiles of the devil, have been *duped* into embracing what Paul referred to as *'a different gospel'*— a 'poverty' gospel that neither aligns with the Jesus depicted in the Bible nor with His actual teachings.

This is precisely what Paul cautioned against:

*For if he who comes preaches another Jesus whom we have not preached, or if you receive a different spirit which you have not received, or **a different gospel which you have not accepted** - you may well put up with it!*

- 2 Corinthians 11:4

*There are some who trouble you and want to **pervert the gospel of Christ**. But even if we, or an angel from heaven, **preach any other gospel to you than what we have preached to you,** let him be accursed.*

- Galatians 1:7-8

THE GOSPEL OF THE KINGDOM IS GOOD NEWS TO THE POOR

There is no greater news for the poor (materially or spiritually) than the restoration of their dignity, inheritance, and divine identity. To that end, God sent His Word to prosper you. However, the widely accepted doctrines and virtues of poverty have led to the emergence of many *Waysiders* who reject the idea that believers can experience wealth, success, influence, and power. To them, such pursuits are often seen as worldly, unspiritual, materialistic, and ungodly. It's no wonder that they struggle to grasp what others joyfully receive, allowing Satan to *snatch* the very Word sown in their hearts.

In describing the spiritual condition of the *'stony heart,'* Jesus underscores the inevitable persecution that arises from receiving the Word of the Kingdom. If the Word sown indeed pertains to wealth, power, and successful living through Christ, it follows that the natural persecutors of those who receive this Word are those whose minds are on the *wayside*.

> **'Waysiders persecute those who want to enter the Kingdom while at the same time are being prevented from entering the Kingdom.'**

This destructive dynamic appears to be a scheme devised by the cunning mind of Satan himself. Therefore, it is essential to *free* the 'Waysiders' from being used as pawns in this scheme, and *everyone* must learn how to stand against Satan. To achieve this, we must first comprehend how Satan snatches away the Word sown in the heart. As mentioned earlier, this can only happen to those already predisposed to the wiles of the enemy, and this predisposition often stems from the **paradigm** they hold.

CHAPTER 24
GET BEHIND ME, SATAN!

"Bring every thought into captivity to the obedience of Christ"

YOUR PARADIGM

In simple terms, your paradigm is a collection of subconscious beliefs that shape your actions and behavior. It serves as the lens through which you perceive the world and your sense of self. To put it colloquially, your paradigm determines whether you see your glass as *'half full or half empty.'* Renowned author and speaker Bob Proctor defines your paradigm as:

'A mental program with almost exclusive control over your behavior.'

He also emphasizes that **all behavior is habitual.** This is a crucial point because there are habits associated with success as well as habits linked to financial hardship. Therefore, paradigms govern both your achievements and your failures.

In his book, The Miseducation of the Negro (one of the most important books ever written on education), Carter G. Woodson underscores the devastating effect of having the wrong paradigm.

*"**If you can control a man's thinking, you do not have to worry about his action.** When you determine what a man shall think, you do not have to concern yourself about what he will do. **If you make a man feel that he is inferior, you do not have to compel him to accept an inferior status, for he will seek it himself.** If you make a man think that he is justly an outcast, you do not have to order him to the back door. **He will go without being told;** and if there is no back door, his very nature will demand one."*

For the most part, your paradigm is not something you consciously originated; rather, it is an accumulation of generational beliefs, often ingrained in the subconscious mind from an early age. As a result, many of the core beliefs that have become the guiding force of our life often come from the habits, customs, and opinions of others. This is especially so when it comes to the subject of money. That is why for many, the subject of money triggers a negative emotion, without a sound reason why. Rather than questioning the beliefs that elicit such feelings, many people rationalize them by hiding behind mental barriers masked as morals, values, ethics, and *even faith!*

Unless these paradigms are addressed, even if they consciously desire success, they will always find themselves torn between moving forward and holding back, much like the analogy Jesus used:

"No one puts a piece from a new garment on an old one; otherwise the new makes a tear, and also the piece that was taken out of the new does not match the old. **And no one puts new wine into old wineskins; or else the new wine will burst the wineskins** *and be spilled, and the wineskins will be ruined.* **But new wine must be put into new wineskins, and both are preserved.***"*
- Matthew 5:36-38

In essence, you cannot embrace a new life of prosperity and abundance with a poverty mindset. Thus, achieving financial freedom starts with adopting a new paradigm!

CAUSE AND EFFECT

In addition to influencing your habitual behavior, paradigms play a significant role in shaping what you presently attract into your life. It may not appear immediately evident, but your paradigm is the root cause of the events that unfold in your life. It's the underlying reason why you consistently experience the same outcomes, whether they are positive or negative, year after year. What you may have interpreted as either good or bad luck can be attributed to your paradigm. In this context, there's no such thing as mere coincidence. Instead, your life follows a precise path guided by the GPS coordinates established by your paradigm.

BLESSED OR CURSED

From a biblical perspective, paradigms are closely intertwined with the concepts of blessings and curses. The Bible illustrates that success in life is less about one's skills or talents and more about whether one is living under a state of blessing or curse. A simple read through Deuteronomy 28 reveals how the principles of blessings and curses encompass every aspect of life, particularly in the realms of health and wealth. This is not to say that skills are of little consequence; on the contrary, it is crucial to commit to honing your skills and striving for excellence in your endeavors. However, many highly talented individuals find themselves broke or failing in key areas of their lives despite their best efforts. Conversely, some individuals with lesser talents seemingly find themselves in the right place at the right time, forming connections with the right people who open doors of opportunity for them.

Jeremiah describes universal principle for the blessing and the curse.

*"**Cursed is the man who trusts in man** and makes flesh his strength, whose heart departs from the Lord. For he shall be like a shrub in the desert, and shall not see when good comes, but shall inhabit the parched places in the wilderness, in a salt land which is not inhabited.*

***Blessed is the man who trusts in the Lord**, and whose hope is the Lord. For he shall be like a tree planted by the waters, which spreads out its roots by the river, and will not fear when heat comes; But its leaf will be green, and will not be anxious in the year of drought, nor will cease from yielding fruit."*

- Jeremiah 17:5-8

The blessing correlates with the abundance mindset, the divine mind of Christ, that empowers one to prosper in all that they put their hand to. This is evident in the life of Joseph, who was described as a prosperous man even while he was a slave. **On the other hand, the curse is linked to the mind of lack and scarcity - the paradigm that undermines divine thinking,** empowering those who hold such mindsets to experience failure or fall short of the life God intends for them to enjoy.

While Jesus' sacrifice on the cross broke the curse that humanity was under, it's crucial to recognize that if your paradigm remains unchanged and doesn't align with God's way of thinking, you might as well still be living under that curse. Hence, Paul urges us all to be **transformed by the renewing of our minds** - renewed to the paradigm of divine thought. In another passage, Paul speaks of being **renewed in the spirit of one's mind,** which is the biblical term for one's paradigm. In essence, your paradigm impacts the quality of your life.

God desires for you to live a life far above your circumstances, while Satan seeks to keep you living far below your privileges and potential. To achieve this, Satan aims to contaminate your mind with *his* way of thinking. This brings us to the subject of how Satan is able to snatch away the Word sown in the heart.

SNATCHING THE WORD

Unlike God, Satan is not omnipresent; he is a finite being who can only be in one place at a time. Therefore, the notion that he *personally* goes around snatching the Word from every individual with a *'wayside'* heart is implausible. Instead, it is Satan's thoughts that perform this act of snatching. Just as there is no distinction between God and His thoughts, there is no separation between Satan and his thoughts. **We, too, become the embodiment of our thoughts.** If Satan's thoughts are imprinted on our subconscious mind, they shape our underlying beliefs. Once this occurs, anything that contradicts those foundational beliefs will be rejected, particularly the Word of the Kingdom.

Just as the act of snatching is quick and abrupt, Satan's thoughts in your mind will lead you to instantly dismiss anything that pertains to the abundant life that God intends for you to enjoy.

> **"BUT WHY WOULD ANY CHRISTIAN ACCEPT SATAN'S THOUGHTS? SURELY, ANY THOUGHT FROM HIM WOULD BE EVIL AND EASY TO REJECT."**

You might be surprised to learn that Satan's thoughts are not always overtly evil. In fact, as a fallen creature, his thinking is very human. Human reasoning often reflects *'fallen thinking,'* which is at odds with the way God thinks. This is why the Bible tells us that God's thoughts are not our thoughts and His ways are not our ways, because His thoughts are 'higher' *(Isaiah 55:8-9)*. However, God doesn't make this distinction to separate His thoughts from ours but rather to underscore how far our thoughts have fallen. Fallen thinking is natural for Satan, while humanity was originally created to think like God.

The Bible also portrays Satan as the *'father of lies,'* and the most effective lie often contain elements of truth. Therefore, it's crucial to know the truth of God's Word and to avoid any departure from it. The more subtle the deviation, the more effective the lie becomes. Even thoughts that may appear good or **well-intentioned** can be considered Satanic if they run counter to God's will. This is why the Bible warns us to guard our hearts with diligence, particularly against those *'well-meaning'* thoughts that can be the most deceptive. You cannot afford to adopt a casual attitude toward the thoughts you entertain, as doing so could be akin to entertaining Satan himself. Jesus was undoubtedly well aware of this reality, as evidenced by His response to Peter's well-intentioned thought.

From that time Jesus began to show to His disciples that He must go to Jerusalem, and suffer many things from the elders and chief priests and scribes, and be killed, and be raised the third day.

Then Peter took Him aside and began to rebuke Him, saying, **"Far be it from You, Lord; this shall not happen to You!"** *But He turned and said to Peter,* **"Get behind Me, Satan!** *You are an offense to Me, for you are not mindful of the things of God, but the things of men."*

- Matthew 16:21-23

At first glance, Jesus' response to Peter's concern about His impending death might seem harsh. After all, Peter was motivated by love for the Lord when he said, *"This shall not happen to You."* However, if Jesus had entertained the thought of avoiding the cross, even for a moment, it would have had catastrophic implications for humanity.

Despite Peter's good intentions and pure motive, he was voicing a Satanic thought! Peter was not *possessed* by Satan. However, since Satan and his thoughts are one, Jesus responded to Peter's words as if He were addressing Satan *in person*. He turned His back to Peter and said,

"Get behind Me, Satan!"

The Wuest New Testament Expanded Translation renders this as,

"Be gone under my authority, and keep on going, behind me, out of my sight, Satan!"

Jesus' response to Peter serves as a powerful example of the mindset and posture we should adopt when confronted with thoughts that oppose God's plan and the Word of the Kingdom, regardless of how well-intentioned they may appear. God sent His Word to prosper you; that is His desire for you. Any thought or belief contrary to you prospering in every aspect of life ultimately stems from a paradigm rooted in Satan's fallen, human-like mind.

SATAN IS AFTER YOUR VISION

To reiterate, your paradigm has almost exclusive control over your life. The divine paradigm empowers you to live a blessed life of success, freedom, joy, peace, health, and wealth. A life where you will prosper at all that you put your hand to and express God's love through your generous giving. Satan, on the other hand, desires to bring you under the curse of *his paradigm*. As the Bible declares, when you are under the curse, **you will not see when good comes.**

"Cursed is the man who trusts in man and makes flesh his strength, whose heart departs from the Lord. For he shall be like a shrub in the desert, **and shall not see when good comes,** *but shall inhabit the parched places in the wilderness, in a salt land which is not inhabited."*

Jeremiah 17:5-6

Satan is after your vision!

He seeks to derail you from your God-given purpose. The well-meaning words he inspired Peter to say to Jesus, was in essence, an attack on His vision and mission. Your vision serves as the blueprint for your life and is the means through which God expresses His will. However, the capacity to see and fulfill your vision can be undermined by the way you think. This is why Satan's primary battleground is the mind, with a particular focus on two key areas of thinking:

Your health and Your wealth.

The absence of good health and financial well-being can significantly hinder you from fulfilling your vision. That's why Satan directs his attacks toward these two crucial areas. It's not surprising that when people are asked which aspect of their lives is most lacking, the most common answers are health or money. These are the areas where many individuals need the most assistance, and this holds true for many Christians as well. Consequently, many Christians fall short of realizing their God-given visions. At best, they achieve a watered-down, diminished, or miniature version of God's grand plan.

Regardless of how purpose-driven or vision-oriented you are, life becomes challenging without the support of good health and financial stability. It's like someone hobbling due to a broken or injured foot, with that pain in one specific area throwing their entire life off balance and into a precarious state. In essence, both wealth and health are not only physical conditions but also states of mind.

RICH AND HEALTHY

> IT IS JUST AS MUCH GOD'S WILL FOR YOU TO BE HEALED IN YOUR FINANCES AS IT IS FOR YOU TO BE HEALED IN YOUR BODY.

I have alluded to the fact that wealth is a paradigm but so too is health. In her best-selling book, *"Who Switched off My Brain,"* Dr. Caroline Leaf reveals research indicating that more than 87% to 98% of illnesses can be attributed to our thought life. Dr. Leaf also discusses the work of pioneering neuroscientist Dr. Candace Pert, who was affectionately known as "The Goddess of Neuroscience" by her admirers. Dr. Pert's work was based on the theory that the body and mind operate as a single psychosomatic network.

Studies have shown that **our thoughts trigger electrochemical reactions in the brain,** which lead to the release of various chemicals based on the emotions associated with those thoughts. Pleasurable thoughts and emotions release endorphins or 'feel-good chemicals,' while painful thoughts and emotions can trigger the release of CRH, also known as the 'negative emotion hormone.' Subsequent stress hormones released in response to CRH can create conditions that contribute to various health problems in the body.

In essence, your thoughts have a profound impact on both the health of your body *and* the balance of your bank account! The devil may have us believe that sickness is a natural part of life, but the truth is that it is anything but natural. Unfortunately, society as a whole has embraced this lie, allowing sickness and disease to become an accepted part of our reality. However, your true identity demands that you live a life of abundance and good health. This is the *natural* way to live, but achieving it often requires a paradigm shift in your thinking.

IN SICKNESS AND IN WEALTH

God does not want you to *hobble* through life but to live a purposeful life marked by divine health and wealth. Just as it is His will for you to be healed in your body, it is also His will for you to be healed in your finances. A powerful example of this principle can be seen in the story of the "Woman with the issue of blood."

When this woman received healing in her body through her faith and determination, Jesus told her, *"Your faith has made you well."* However, He didn't stop there. He also said, *"Go in peace and be healed of your affliction!"*

This might raise the question,

"IF SHE WAS ALREADY MADE WELL BY HER FAITH, WHAT AFFLICTION WAS LEFT TO BE HEALED?"

The answer lies in the circumstances surrounding her healing. She spent all that she had on many physicians and was now *broke!* Although she had the faith to obtain what she desired, she only went as far as her physical condition! Maybe, like many, she did not believe that God would restore her finances just as easily as He would restore her health. Thankfully, Jesus recognized both her bodily disease and financial lack as *'afflictions'* and took the opportunity to heal her in both aspects of her life.

God is love!

He cares about every facet of your life, not just the parts *you choose* to focus on. Therefore, your health and your wealth are of *equal* importance to Him. That is why He wishes *above all things* that you prosper and be in health *(3 John 1:2)*. However, the key to living in perpetual health and wealth is to have a *prosperous* soul and mind.

BREAKING THE CURSE

Like leaven that affects the whole batch of dough, it only takes a seemingly well-meaning *thought-seed* from Satan to profoundly impact your entire life, setting you on an endless cycle of defeat. This becomes especially true when these thoughts become deeply entrenched in your subconscious mind, forming fortresses or strongholds within your mind. Thus, it's essential to heed the guidance of the apostle Paul on dealing with specific trains of thought.

For the weapons of our warfare are not carnal but mighty in God for pulling down strongholds, **casting down arguments and every high thing that exalts itself against the knowledge of God***, bringing every thought into captivity to the obedience of Christ, and being ready to punish all disobedience when your obedience is fulfilled.*

- 2 Corinthians 10:4-6

The arguments and *'high things'* Paul speaks of include those *self-righteous opinions* that seem to claim a higher moral ground than God's Word. These are the type of thoughts that must be pulled down and brought into captivity to the obedience of Christ. For instance,

God sent His Word to prosper you! Therefore, in the same way Jesus brought down every thought seeking to come between Him and the cross, you too must bring down every *high-minded* thought, seeking to come between you and the prosperous life God wants you to live.

'Bring them all into captivity by executing your God-given authority over the author of such opinions.'

If you are a Kingdom-minded person, who is serious about having, not just personal wealth, but **generational wealth**, I am sure you have probably been confronted with these opinions or even criticized by *Waysiders* for desiring such wealth! These opinions are the usual response given by critics whenever it comes to the subject of wealth, prosperity, and having the good you desire.

I urge you not to allow yourself to be indicted by such opinions or made to feel guilty. Instead, follow Jesus' example and **command Satan to get behind you!!** *Whether you choose to speak this command audibly or silently is a matter of your discretion.* Keep in mind that when you issue this command, you are addressing Satan directly, not *the person* influenced by these opinions. Always remember that your true adversary is Satan, and your mission should be to love and support your fellow brothers and sisters.

Here are the most common statements deserving of the response - 'Get behind Me Satan' accompanied with a fitting rebuttal:

"Money is not everything"
- "Get behind Me, Satan"

Rebuttal: Working 8-12 hours a day, 5-6 days a week for money is more indicative of money being *'everything.'* Exchanging large amounts of your time for money, robs you of quality time with God, your spouse, and your family. Prosperity and financial freedom break the grip of money on your life, allowing you to enjoy a more balanced and fulfilling life where money isn't the central focus or overwhelming need.

"Money is the root of all evil"
- "Get behind Me, Satan!"

Rebuttal: It's essential to remember that it's the *love* of money that's described as the root of all evil, not money itself. In many cases, it's the *lack* of money that causes division and strife. Money, in essence, is a resource for goodness and empowerment when in the hands of those whose heart is towards God.

"You could have sold this and give to the poor"
- "Get behind Me, Satan!"

Rebuttal: Kingdom-minded individuals do not think in terms of lack. Much like Christ, they perceive life through the lens of heaven's reality, where the concept of lack and insufficiency does not exist. They know how to *'buy without money'* and manifest the good they desire from the abundant resources of the Kingdom within. In this context, the assertion, *"You could have sold this and given to the poor,"* has no merit because what I or any other believer have does not diminish the abundance available to you!

Jesus only told the rich young ruler to sell what he had and give to the poor to enable him to undergo the paradigm shift required for him to enter into the realm of unlimited resources where he could have whatever he desired through total trust in God.

"I just want to be comfortable and have enough for myself"
- *"Get behind Me, Satan!"*

Rebuttal: You have a divine responsibility to love your neighbor as yourself – this is the Royal Law! You cannot give to others and help them financially if you only have enough for yourself. The notion of only desiring enough for yourself might seem like a selfless stance, however, not only is this selfish, but it is also worse than greed! Christ instructs us to give to those who ask, **'hoping for nothing in return!'** This is the nature of God's children. You can't very well do that if you are always broke!

These sentiments and more are no different from the false indignation displayed by Judas when he considered the act of pouring expensive oil on Jesus' head as wasteful! They are all offensive terms, befitting the response - "Get behind Me, Satan!"

You are more valuable to God than you can ever imagine.

**No amount of money can equal your worth.
The King of Kings lives in you, working through you and as you.**

Therefore, wealth, riches, and power are the most appropriate things for you to have.

There is no such thing as excess or extravagance when it comes to honoring your divine worth.

─────◆─────

THE DECISION

"This day I call the heavens and the earth as witnesses against you that I have set before you life and death"

To choose CHRIST is to choose LIFE.
Not an ordinary life but a rich trichotomy of
purpose, power, and destiny.

It is life at the highest level of living brought about
by the highest level of thinking.
Where dire circumstances can be changed rather than be accepted.
Where impossibilities are merely the product of unbelief and
possibilities are subject to that which we choose to believe.
This is the *'everlasting life'* that God promised.

Everlasting life is the divine right of those who
dare to identify themselves with Christ.
The identity we lost in Adam but regained in Christ.

Everlasting life is not life after death but life despite death,
thanks to 'The One' who conquered death.

To choose Christ is to choose dominion.
You were created to have dominion on the earth.
That means you are supposed to have dominion over anything that
challenges your wellbeing and the wellbeing of others.
Whether it's in the area of your finances, health, career, relationships,
or spiritual growth, in Christ, you have dominion over them all.

When you choose Christ,
you will stand and shine in your uniqueness,
rather than sit on the bench of commonality.
Your uniqueness is the solution
to the needs of a specific set of people.
Your uniqueness is linked to the gifts and talents
that God meticulously wove into your divine make up.

We were all created with particular gifts and talents.
Some are discovered early in life, and others much later.
Often times we either sit on our talents or put them to improper use.
Only a few are fortunate enough to make a global impact with their
gift, and fewer still manage to find the true purpose of their gift.
Only in Christ do your gifts, talents, and uniqueness find their
purpose, bringing you to your place of influence.

In your place of influence you are strategically positioned to positively
impact the world, or to prevent the outcome of a dire situation.

That is your purpose.
That is your destiny.

We saw this in the life of Joseph, whose unique gifting was in
the area of dreams and the interpretation of them.
Although his gift led to him being sold into slavery by his brothers,
his gift also brought him to a place of prominence and influence.
It was his influence that saved the lives of millions from a dire
situation, *including the lives of his brothers.*
That was his destiny.

The world is waiting for your divine light to shine!
This can only be achieved in Christ,
where you meet your 'Ultimate Self.'

Thank you for taking the time to
read Jesus Was A Billionaire.
Your support means the world to me.

If you enjoyed this book and it was a blessing to you,
I would be immensely grateful if you could take
a moment to **leave a review.**

Your feedback allows other readers
to discover this work.

OTHER BOOKS BY
THE AUTHOR

Vision - Seeing Is Achieving
AVAILABLE FROM AMAZON

Are you searching for clarity and direction in your life?
Are you stuck at the crossroads of faith and ambition,
yearning to discover your true calling?

*"Embark on a transformative journey guided by faith
and the power of vision."*

From understanding the true nature of the universe to applying mental laws
that shape your reality, this book is a comprehensive guide to:
Understanding and harnessing the power of your mind and vision.
Manifest your goals and unleash your creative power.
See beyond the limitations of your circumstances.

Ultimately, 'Vision - Seeing is Achieving" provides the tools
and wisdom to unleash your potential, transform your 'big dream'
into reality, and live a purpose-driven life.

Wisdom Brings Success
AVAILABLE FROM AMAZON

Wisdom Brings Success will open your eyes to possibilities and realities that will renew your thinking and transform your life.

In this book you will find valuable insights and wisdom that will not only cause you to see beyond barriers, but also break the barriers that hinder your success.

Wisdom Brings Success is the result of in-depth study in the art of excellence, by author, inspirational speaker and serial entrepreneur, Allan Sealy. Due to his extensive business and coaching experience, Allan is able to present practical lessons on life mastery from a unique perspective.

www.ingramcontent.com/pod-product-compliance
Lightning Source LLC
Chambersburg PA
CBHW030904080526
44589CB00010B/136